MW00949228

# EXCEL BEGINNER TO MASTER

# Table of Contents

# Table of Contents (continued)

# Table of Contents (continued)

# Table of Contents (continued)

# Module 1

- Introduction
- Getting Acclimated
- Opening Microsoft Excel
- Saving Files

# Module 1: Introduction

Microsoft Excel is a spreadsheet application that is used for storing, organizing and analyzing data.

This course is designed to build the participant's skill set and confidence as it pertains to the practical application of the software's tools and features. We will start with an overview of fundamentals where we will focus on the "what and how" of the individual components. As we transition through the course, the emphasis will be on tying it all together to effectively use Microsoft Excel through practice examples.

Whether this is your first time working with Microsoft Excel or you have experience, it is highly recommended that you dive in and work with it. You will develop your own style and techniques which you will continue to develop and hone. You will most likely interact with other users and pick up tricks and techniques along the way. Remember everyone once opened the program for the first time!

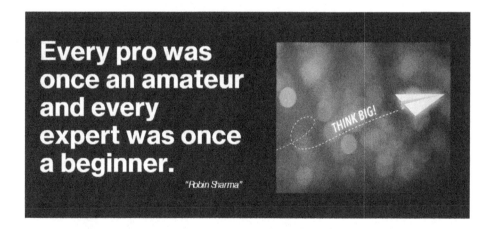

# Section 2: Getting Acclimated

In this section, the focus will be on getting acclimated to the program and learning how to navigate around some of the key areas.

As Microsoft continues to improve and update Excel, each revision is given a new version number. For example, Excel 2021, 2019, 2016, 365 and so on. Depending on your version some of the icons and layout may look slightly different than the ones used in the examples and demonstrations.

This workbook is designed to compliment the video tutorials and it is intended that you work along in your live application.

**Opening Microsoft Excel and Saving Files:** Three (3) different methods will be reviewed on how to open the application. We will start by checking if the computer has Microsoft Excel installed. A helpful technique, called "pinning" will be demonstrated. Lastly, a file will be saved, and a desktop shortcut will be created to that file

1. Checking if it is installed on the computer
2. Pinning to Taskbar
3. Creating Desktop Shortcut after Saving the file

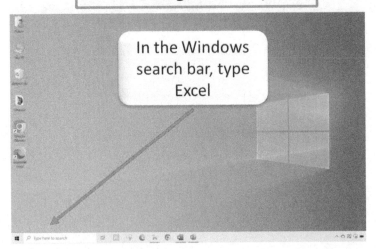

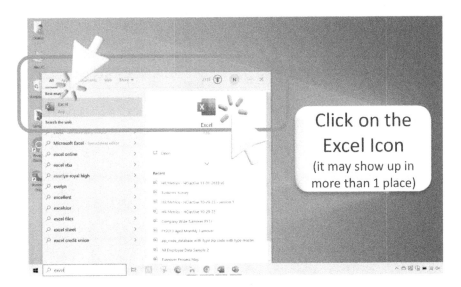

The Excel screen will open and click on "Blank Workbook"

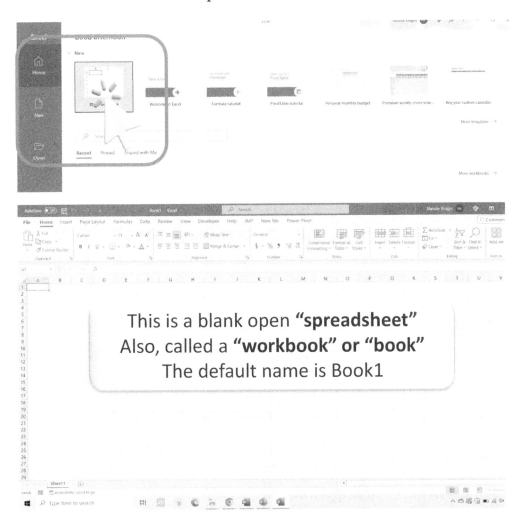

# To Save:

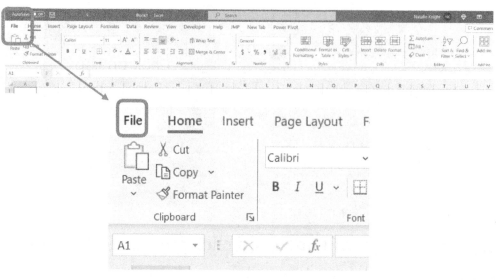

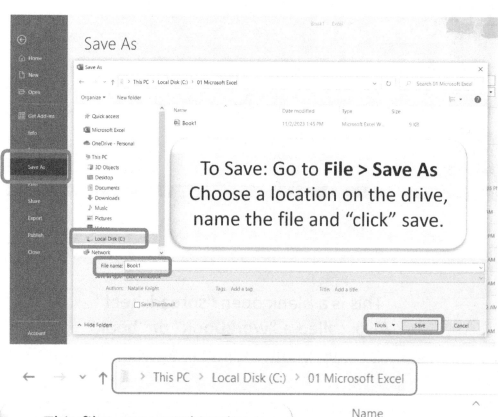

To Save: Go to **File > Save As**
Choose a location on the drive,
name the file and "click" save.

This file was saved in the
highlighted location and the
filename is 'Saving Example"

Name

Saving Example

## 2. Creating Desktop Shortcut

From the file location in the directory, a desktop shortcut can be made for easy access directly to the file.

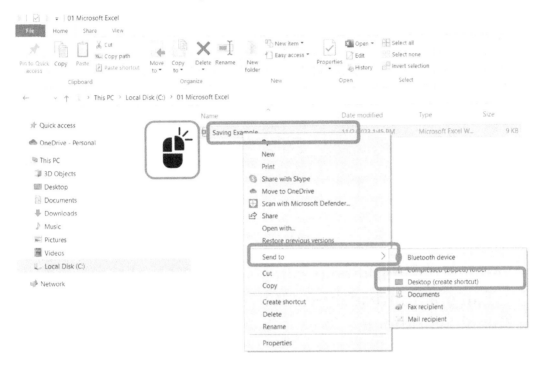

"Right Click" on the filename and "Click" **Send to > Desktop Create Shortcut**

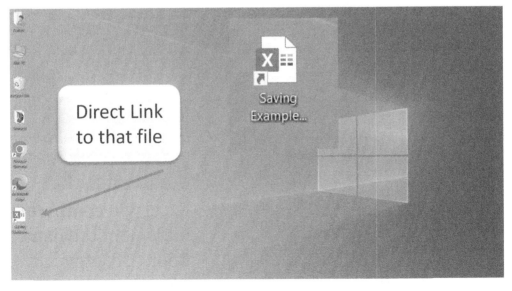

To move to another location on the desktop, "Left Click" drag to the location, and release.

Additional workbooks can also be opened from inside of an open spreadsheet. "Click" File and then on the blank workbook.

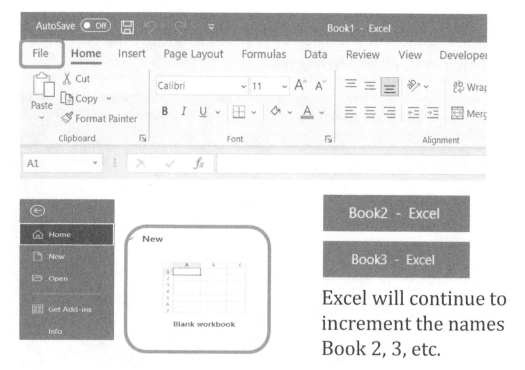

Excel will continue to increment the names Book 2, 3, etc.

There are 2 types of "Saving":
1. Save
2. Save As

Save – will save the file with the current name, in the current location. This will save over top of the last changes.

Save As – creates a copy of the file and the name can be changed. If the name is not changed, Excel will give a message that the file already exists. (see next page)

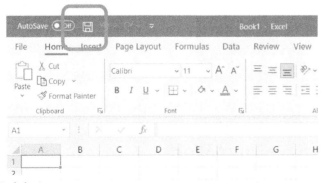

The little "save" icon also performs the same function as "save"

The image below shows how the files show up on the drive and the message indicating that Book 1 is going to be replaced by the new version.

Other helpful information is the date / time last modified, file type and size.

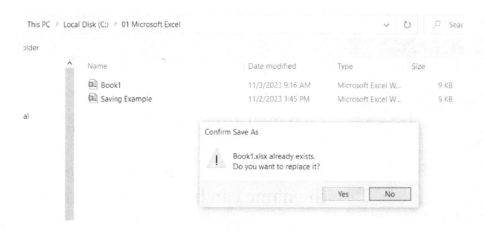

## Summary: Module 1

Following a brief course overview, different methods for opening the Microsoft Excel application were reviewed. Creating a shortcut to a file, as well as pinning to the taskbar was shown. It is usually a personal preference on which method is best to use. The important process, for file saving was covered and it is helpful to develop a good method for organizing, naming, and saving your work!

**To Save Your Work!**

# Module 2

- Ribbon
- Tabs
- Sheet Information
- Layout
- Basic Operations
- Short Cut Keys

# The Ribbon and Spreadsheet Layout

The" Ribbon" in Microsoft Excel is the top portion of the spreadsheet where different tasks, commands, and operations can be accessed. As the ribbon can be customized by users, the actual tabs may be different from the example shown. In this section, we will go through the different toolbars and tabs and review some of the key functionality.

Below highlights the general layout of the Ribbon:

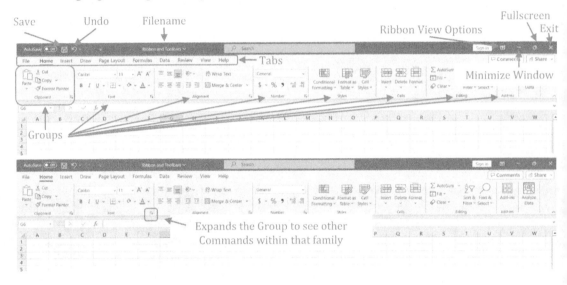

Below highlights the general layout of the Spreadsheet:

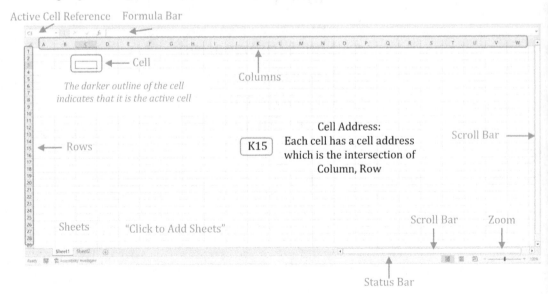

# General Sheet Information

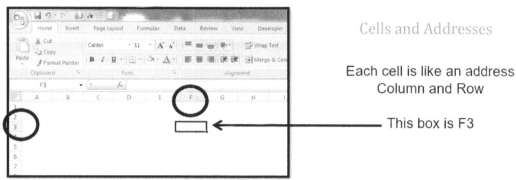

### Cells and Addresses

Each cell is like an address
Column and Row

This box is F3

## Selecting: Cells, Multiple Cells, Entire Row or Entire Column

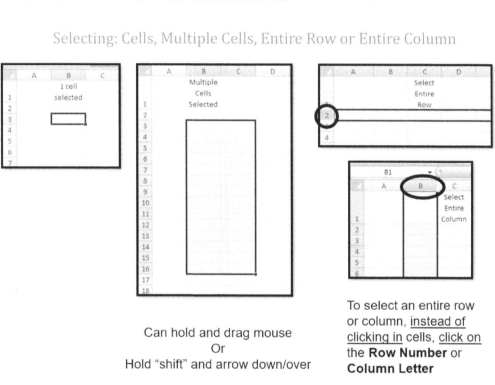

Can hold and drag mouse
Or
Hold "shift" and arrow down/over

To select an entire row
or column, instead of
clicking in cells, click on
the **Row Number** or
**Column Letter**

## Excel Total Rows and Columns

### 1,048,576 rows        16,384 columns

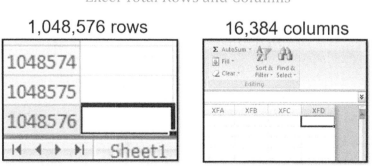

# General Formula and Calculation Basics

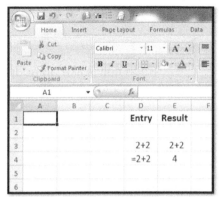

### "Telling" Excel to calculate

= tells Excel that you want it to calculate or perform the function of a formula

## Formula Basics: Entering numbers vs Formulas

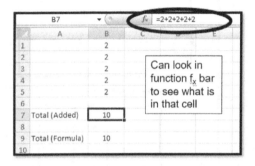

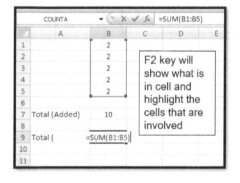

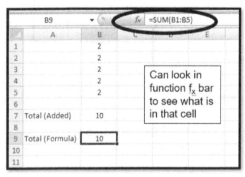

Formulas will allow for updating when numbers change

## Parenthesis Impact Formula Calculations

| | A | B | C | | E | F | G | H | I | J | K | L |
|---|---|---|---|---|---|---|---|---|---|---|---|---|
| 1 | | | | Formula Bar | | | | | | | | |
| 2 | | 2 | 10 | 5 | | 8 | | | =(B2*C2)/D2+4 | | | |
| 3 | | | | | | | | | | | | |
| 4 | | 2 | 10 | 5 | | 2.2 | | | =((B4*C4)/(D4+4)) | | | |
| 5 | | | | | | | | | | | | |
| 6 | | | | | | | | | | | | |

# General Formula Information (continued)

## Common Formulas

The f$_x$ button will show the list of formulas

It is possible to search for formulas

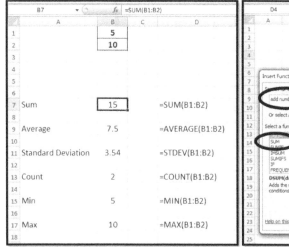

## "Freezing" Formulas: Absolute and Relative Reference

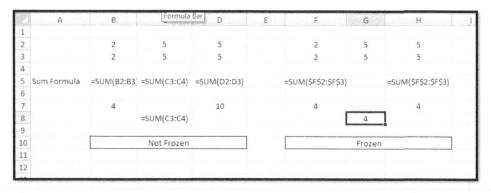

# General Formatting Information

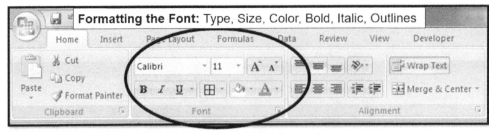

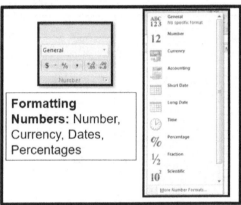

## Format Alignment

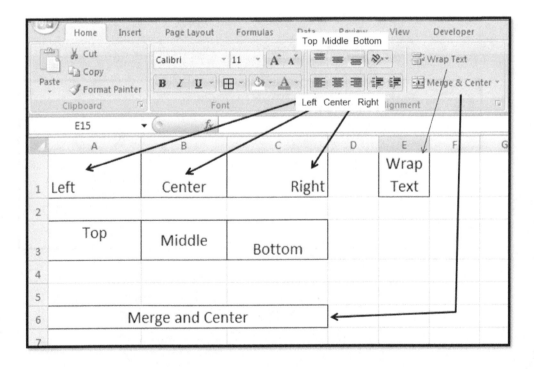

# General Formatting (Continued)

## Copy, Paste Format Painter

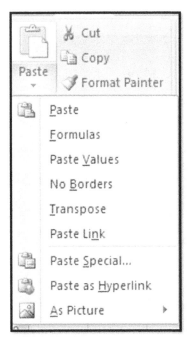

- Removes content of cells
- Copies content of cells, including formulas
- Copies the format of the cell
- Puts what is copied or cut in the designated cell

- Put the value that is in the cell instead of the formulas

- Converts horizontal to vertical and vice versa

- Allows for a combination of pasting options

**Short Cut Keys**
Ctrl C = Copy
Ctrl V = Paste
Ctrl X = Cut

## Deleting and Inserting

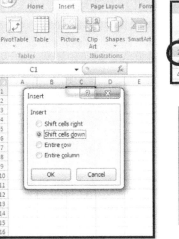

"Right" Click Insert / Delete brings up window    OR

Select entire row / column and "right" click insert / delete

# General Sheet Information

## Freezing Panes

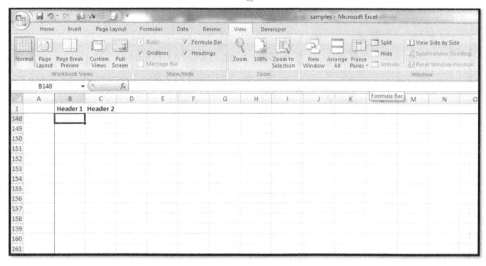

Can freeze at rows and columns to allow scrolling with headers visible

## Managing Sheets

"Click" + to Add Sheets

"Right Click" + to see manage sheet options

- Insert *(new can also be done from here)*
- Delete
- Rename
- Move or Copy (can also drag to move)
- Change Color
- Hide

When copying, make sure to check "create a copy" and choose the location same workbook or new.

Module 2

# Shortcut Keys (Ctrl + Key)

| KEY | DESCRIPTION |
| --- | --- |
| CTRL+PgUp | Switches between worksheet tabs, from left-to-right. |
| CTRL+PgDn | Switches between worksheet tabs, from right-to-left. |
| CTRL+SHIFT+( | Unhides any hidden rows within the selection. |
| CTRL+SHIFT+) | Unhides any hidden columns within the selection. |
| CTRL+SHIFT+& | Applies the outline border to the selected cells. |
| CTRL+SHIFT_ | Removes the outline border from the selected cells. |
| CTRL+SHIFT+~ | Applies the General number format. |
| CTRL+SHIFT+$ | Applies the Currency format with two decimal places (negative numbers in parentheses). |
| CTRL+SHIFT+% | Applies the Percentage format with no decimal places. |
| CTRL+SHIFT+^ | Applies the Exponential number format with two decimal places. |
| CTRL+SHIFT+# | Applies the Date format with the day, month, and year. |
| CTRL+SHIFT+@ | Applies the Time format with the hour and minute, and AM or PM. |
| CTRL+SHIFT+! | Applies the Number format with two decimal places, thousands separator, and minus sign (-) for negative values. |
| CTRL+SHIFT+* | Selects the current region around the active cell (the data area enclosed by blank rows and blank columns). In a PivotTable, it selects the entire PivotTable report. |
| CTRL+SHIFT+: | Enters the current time. |
| CTRL+SHIFT+" | Copies the value from the cell above the active cell into the cell or the Formula Bar. |
| CTRL+SHIFT+Plus (+) | Displays the **Insert** dialog box to insert blank cells. |
| CTRL+Minus (-) | Displays the **Delete** dialog box to delete the selected cells. |
| CTRL+; | Enters the current date. |
| CTRL+` | Alternates between displaying cell values and displaying formulas in the worksheet. |
| CTRL+' | Copies a formula from the cell above the active cell into the cell or the Formula Bar. |
| CTRL+1 | Displays the **Format Cells** dialog box. |
| CTRL+2 | Applies or removes bold formatting. |
| CTRL+3 | Applies or removes italic formatting. |
| CTRL+4 | Applies or removes underlining. |
| CTRL+5 | Applies or removes strikethrough. |

# Shortcut Keys (Continued)

| | |
|---|---|
| CTRL+6 | Alternates between hiding objects, displaying objects, and displaying placeholders for objects. |
| CTRL+8 | Displays or hides the outline symbols. |
| CTRL+9 | Hides the selected rows. |
| CTRL+0 | Hides the selected columns. |
| CTRL+A | Selects the entire worksheet. |
| | If the worksheet contains data, CTRL+A selects the current region. Pressing CTRL+A a second time selects the current region and its summary rows. Pressing CTRL+A a third time selects the entire worksheet. |
| | When the insertion point is to the right of a function name in a formula, displays the **Function Arguments** dialog box. |
| | CTRL+SHIFT+A inserts the argument names and parentheses when the insertion point is to the right of a function name in a formula. |
| CTRL+B | Applies or removes bold formatting. |
| CTRL+C | Copies the selected cells. |
| | CTRL+C followed by another CTRL+C displays the Clipboard. |
| CTRL+D | Uses the **Fill Down** command to copy the contents and format of the topmost cell of a selected range into the cells below. |
| CTRL+F | Displays the **Find and Replace** dialog box, with the **Find** tab selected. |
| | SHIFT+F5 also displays this tab, while SHIFT+F4 repeats the last Find action. |
| | CTRL+SHIFT+F opens the **Format Cells** dialog box with the **Font** tab selected. |
| CTRL+G | Displays the **Go To** dialog box. |
| | F5 also displays this dialog box. |
| CTRL+H | Displays the **Find and Replace** dialog box, with the **Replace** tab selected. |
| CTRL+I | Applies or removes italic formatting. |
| CTRL+K | Displays the **Insert Hyperlink** dialog box for new hyperlinks or the **Edit Hyperlink** dialog box for selected existing hyperlinks. |
| CTRL+N | Creates a new, blank workbook. |
| CTRL+O | Displays the **Open** dialog box to open or find a file. |
| | CTRL+SHIFT+O selects all cells that contain comments. |

Module 2

# Shortcut Keys (Continued)

| | |
|---|---|
| CTRL+H | Displays the **Find and Replace** dialog box, with the **Replace** tab selected. |
| CTRL+I | Applies or removes italic formatting |
| CTRL+K | Displays the **Insert Hyperlink** dialog box for new hyperlinks or the **Edit Hyperlink** dialog box for selected existing hyperlinks. |
| CTRL+N | Creates a new, blank workbook |
| CTRL+O | Displays the **Open** dialog box to open or find a file. |
| | CTRL+SHIFT+O selects all cells that contain comments. |
| CTRL+P | Displays the **Print** dialog box. |
| | CTRL+SHIFT+P opens the **Format Cells** dialog box with the Font tab selected. |
| CTRL+R | Uses the **Fill Right** command to copy the contents and format of the leftmost cell of a selected range into the cells to the right. |
| CTRL+S | Saves the active file with its current file name, location, and file format. |
| CTRL+T | Displays the **Create Table** dialog box. |
| CTRL+U | Applies or removes underlining |
| | CTRL+SHIFT+U switches between expanding and collapsing of the formula bar. |
| CTRL+V | Inserts the contents of the Clipboard at the insertion point and replaces any selection. Available only after you have cut or copied an object, text, or cell contents. |
| | CTRL+ALT+V displays the **Paste Special** dialog box. Available only after you have cut or copied an object, text, or cell contents on a worksheet or in another program. |
| CTRL+W | Closes the selected workbook window. |
| CTRL+X | Cuts the selected cells. |
| CTRL+Y | Repeats the last command or action, if possible. |
| CTRL+Z | Uses the **Undo** command to reverse the last command or to delete the last entry that you typed. |
| | CTRL+SHIFT+Z uses the **Undo** or **Redo** command to reverse or restore the last automatic correction when AutoCorrect Smart Tags are displayed. |

⬆ TOP OF PAGE

# Summary: Module 2

In this module and overview of the basic spreadsheet layout was provided. The structure of the file is workbook or spreadsheet and each separate page within the spreadsheet is a sheet. The default sheet names are sheet 1,2,3, and so on. The sheet names can be changed by right clicking and choosing rename. This can also be accessed by double clicking. There is a character limit on the length of a sheet name of thirty-one. (31) Sheets can be copied within the same file, moved by dragging to another location order or by right clicking and selecting move or copy. By checking the check box "create a copy" a copy of the sheet is created. To have the destination of that copy go to another file, select the drop down and chose the destination file or select the new book. The sheet tabs can also be colored.

The Ribbon is the main tool bar and menu section of Microsoft Excel. The different tabs represent groups of like functions and commands. There are many options available and little arrows will expand that section into more options. It is advised to navigate and practice within the different menus. There are often descriptions and guides available when hovering on different icons. To customize and add to the ribbon and toolbar go to File > Options > Customize Ribbon. This will show what commands are already in the tool bar and the other available options that can be added.

Each cell has a row and column reference that indicates its address. This address is used in formulas and source data for various functions. It is possible to select a singe cell, group of cells or entire rows and columns.

There is a variety of formatting options that include color, size, fonts, font emphasis, as well as positioning within a cell.

Many operations can be performed with a mouse or keyboard. There are several short cut key combinations that can help speed up some of the routine operations.

Freezing panes allows for scrolling on the page while leaving the "frozen" areas visible which helps when navigating around larger sheets.

There is a wide list of formulas and calculations that help facilitate summarizing and analysis. They are initiated by = sign and have helper text to support the format of the formula. Formulas can be copied to other cells and the address reference will shift to the corresponding position. This can be controlled by using $ and is called absolute and relative reference. This is applicable to both row numbers and column letters. Putting the $ in front of the address component will freeze it to current value and is an absolute reference. No matter where the formula is copied to when it has an absolute reference it will continue to point to the same location specified by the $.

# Module 3

- Working through the Tabs

# Section 2: The File Tab

This section will demonstrate some of the operations within the "File" tab.

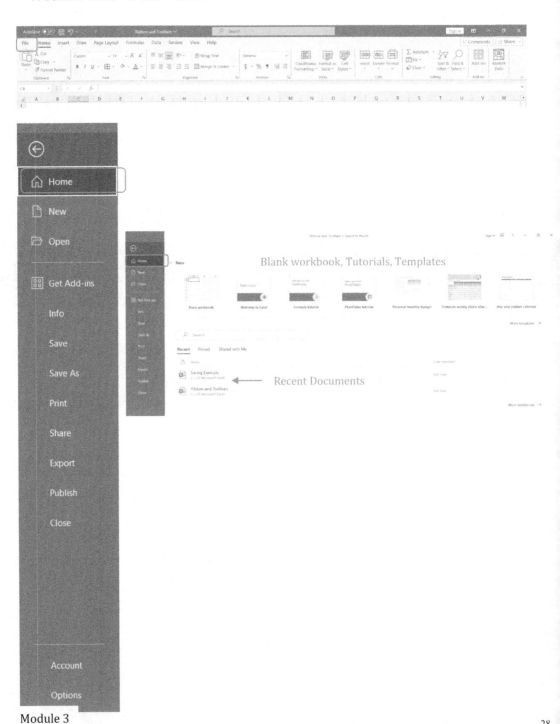

The "New" menu allows for creating a brand-new spreadsheet. This menu is great because it shows some helpful templates that can help inspire a format.

The search bar can also be used to look for a template online.

The "Open" menu allows for opening another Excel file from within the Excel application. The drives can be searched, or the file can be opened from the list of recently opened files.

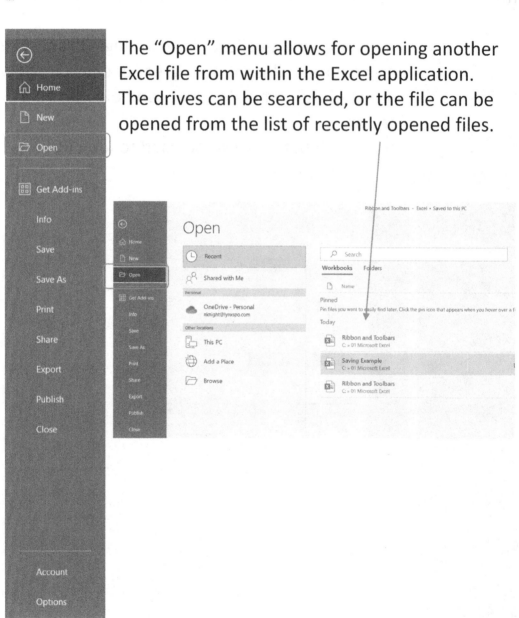

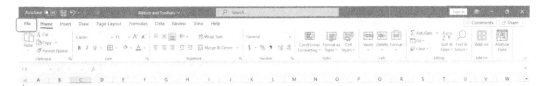

The "Add-ins" are a place where more features and options can be added to Microsoft Excel. We will work with add-ins later throughout the course.

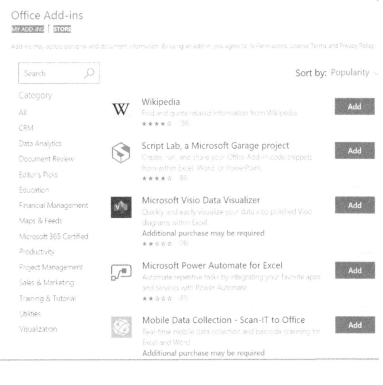

# "Info" contains aspects related to the file properties, location and is the section where a password can be added upon opening.

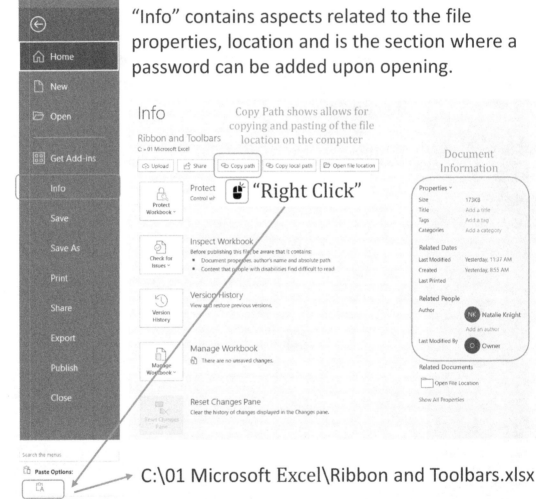

Info

Copy Path shows allows for copying and pasting of the file location on the computer

C:\01 Microsoft Excel\Ribbon and Toolbars.xlsx

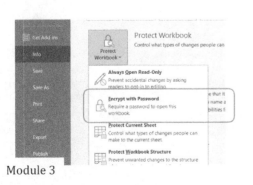

"Right Click" Paste

---

## A password to open the file can be entered.

The Save and Save As commands are within this menu as well as the Print Setup which we will work with later in the course.

The "Options" is a place to access, view, and adjust various settings. There are different categories of settings within one menu location.

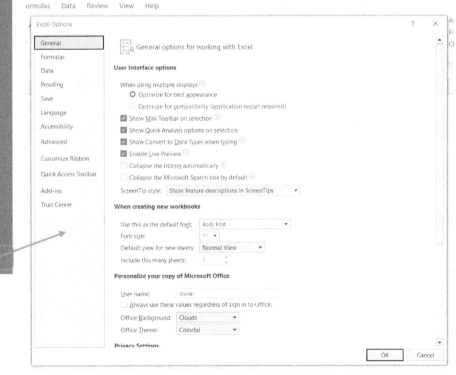

# Section 3: Overview of Tab Content

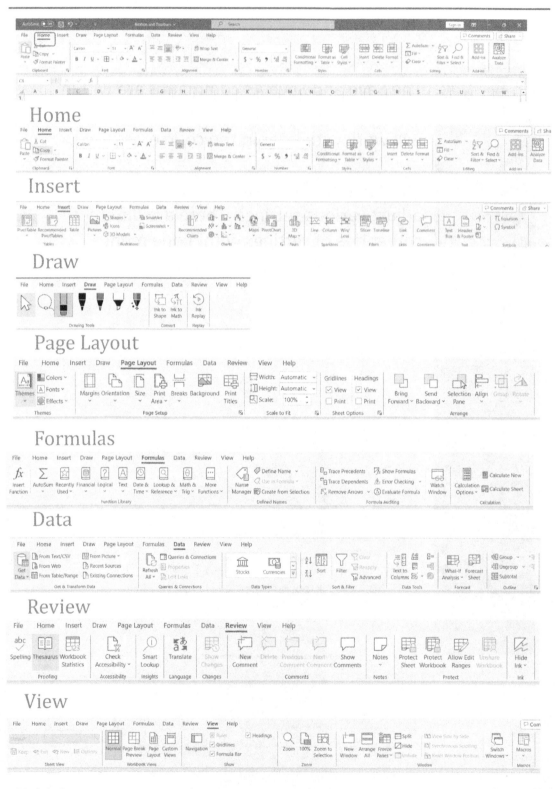

## Home

## Insert

## Draw

## Page Layout

## Formulas

## Data

## Review

## View

# Summary: Module 3

In this module the focus was on getting orientated with the tabs on the ribbon. The File Tab has functionality related to file opening, saving and printing. There is an option in this menu to protect the workbook and put a password on the file. This is helpful for sensitive information or to protect the file from accidental changes.

There are two place in which to install Add Ins. Add Ins can help extend functionality across other platforms as well as enhance current capabilities.

The Home Tab houses most of the formatting options. This includes cell color, font color, font type, size, and enhancements. The copy past icon has the icons for the basic functions visible including Format Painter. Format Painter allows of cell format to be transferred to other cells. Single click of the format painter allows for a single application or "swipe" of that format in a single cell or across multiple cells. Double Clicking on the format painter allows for transferring the format to multiple cells with separate actions. Format painter also works for formats set with conditional formatting.

The Alignment Tab allows for positioning the cell contents in different ways. It is possible to Left, Right and Center Justify the text horizontal, as well as, setting the orientation vertically with top middle bottom. The text direction options allow for the text to be rotated and wrap text will allow for the text to fit within a cell that has a width shorter than the length of the text. This is especially helpful for longer, more descriptive headers when the cell content value is narrower. Using formats in combination can really help improve the appearance and organization of the spreadsheet.

There is also a feature called Merge and Center. This allows for multiple cells being combined together so that cell contents can be positioned. This is great to use for titles or additional formatting that adds to organization and appearance. It is important to pay attention to the cell's address when merged. It will take on the address of the first cell. The cell address can be referenced and verified by checking the address bar in the top left corner right under the ribbon groups. Both columns and rows can be merged.

Conditional formatting allows for setting format based on criteria vs static formatting. This can be used to enhance visualizations or call attention to specific values. There is a built-in feature that can highlight duplicates. Color scales and icon sets are within the conditional formatting menu. The formatting can be cleared in this menu and all of the format's set can be reviewed in the manage rule option.

# Module 4

- Practice Files
- Ribbons and Tabs

# Lesson 1: Practice Sheet

Filename: 1 Practice Sheet Module 3

Sheet: Lesson 1 Home

| Practice Actions | | |
|---|---|---|
| 1. Enter "Green" in G1 & "Yellow" in H1 | | |
| 2. Select all colors - E1 to H1 & Click Copy | | |
| 3. Paste the colors in row 2 | | |
| 4. Highlight E2 to H2 and click the "delete" | Delete | |
| 5. Highlight E1 to H1 and click "cut" | | |
| 6. Move down 1 row and click paste in E2 | | |
| 7. Highlight E2 to H2 and click the "B" in font group. To Make the headers bold. | B | |
| 8. Practice clicking on the italics & underline and then return it to bold only | *I* <u>U</u> | |
| 9. Select E1 (Red) & Change the Font to **Wide Latin** | | |
| 10. Practice increasing and decreasing font size & leave the font size of "Red" to 14 | | |
| 11. While in cell E2 (Red), "Double Click" the "Format Painter" icon. Then swipe it over the cells containing Blue, Green, & Yellow | Format Painter | |
| 12. Practice expanding column widths for columns E, F, G, H: Single Column, Auto Size & Highlight all columns together | | |
| 13. Center the Font inside of the cell | | |
| 14. Color the Red, Blue cells (Red & Blue), for Green & Yellow format cells gray and font the color of the word (Green, Yellow) | A | |
| 15. Enter the number of beads in the jar to the corresponding cell; center in cell | | |

# Lesson 1: Practice Sheet - Completed

| Red | Blue | Green | Yellow |
|:---:|:---:|:---:|:---:|
| 3 | 2 | 4 | 5 |

Lesson 1 provided practice steps within the "Home" tab of the Ribbon.

| Jar of Beads | Practice Actions |
|---|---|
| A simple example will be utilized to put spreadsheet functions into action | 1. Enter "Green" in G1 & "Yellow" in H1 |
| | 2. Select all colors - E1 to H1 & Click Copy |
| | 3. Paste the colors in row 2 |
| | 4. Highlight E2 to H2 and click the "delete" |
| | 5. Highlight E1 to H1 and click "cut" |
| | 6. Move down 1 row and click paste in E2 |
| | 7. Highlight E2 to H2 and click the "B" in font group. To Make the headers bold. |
| | 8. Practice clicking on the italics & underline and then return it to bold only |
| | 9. Select E1 (Red) & Change the Font to **Wide Latin** |
| | 10. Practice increasing and decreasing font size & leave the font size of "Red" to 14 |
| | 11. While in cell E2 (Red), "Double Click" the "Format Painter" icon. Then swipe it over the cells containing Blue, Green, & |
| | 12. Practice expanding column widths for columns E, F, G, H: Single Column, Auto Size & Highlight all columns together |
| | 13. Center the Font inside of the cell |
| | 14. Color the Red, Blue cells (Red & Blue), for Green & Yellow format cells gray and font the color of the word (Green, Yellow) |
| | 15. Enter the number of beads in the jar to the corresponding cell; center in cell |

# Lesson 2: Practice Sheet

Filename: 1 Practice Sheet Module 3

Sheet: Lesson 2

1. Reformat the Colors to Times New Roman font size 12

2. Delete the numbers in E2 to H2

3. Add a date column and enter the data

4. Format, Center, Bold Date (D2)

5. Select E3 to H7 and Center numbers

6. Select D1 to H1 - Merge and Center

7. Type Jar of Beads Colors Data in D1

8. Bold Title

9. Highlight Dates (D3 to D7) - change to long  date format

10. Click Undo and Redo

11. Select all data E3 to E7. Go to Conditional Formatting > Highlight Cell Rules > Duplicate Values

12. Change the date to M/DD format. Number format and more number formats.

13. Select the entire table D2 to H7 and go to Format as Table and select the first option in "medium"

14. Select all of the numbers E3:H7 and click Auto Sum

15. Select E3 to E7 and look at status bar for totals

# Lesson 2: Completed

| Jar of Beads Colors Data | | | | |
|---|---|---|---|---|
| **Date** | **Red** | **Blue** | **Green** | **Yellow** |
| 1/1 | 5 | 4 | 1 | 1 |
| 1/5 | 4 | 3 | 1 | 2 |
| 1/10 | 10 | 1 | 1 | 3 |
| 1/12 | 5 | 2 | 2 | 1 |
| 1/15 | 2 | 3 | 3 | 3 |
| | **26** | **13** | **8** | **10** |

Lesson 2 allowed for manual data entry processes, table formatting, conditional formatting.

# Lesson 3: Practice Sheet

Filename: 1 Practice Sheet Module 3

Sheet: Lesson 3 Home and Insert

1.  Select D1 to I16 and format with a border

2. Select E1 to H1 and click Auto Sum

3. Review the formula that it placed in I2

4. Select I2, Copy and Paste to Cell I 3 to I16

5. Review how the formula adjusted for the row.

6. Center and Bold the totals in cell, click arrow and ignore error message

7. Select Total Beads Column I1 to I17, Click Insert > Recommended Charts (Select the first bar chart)

8. Select the chart and move, drag the corners to resize it to fit on the screen

9. Select the chart and Click Chart Design

10. Click Select Data > Edit (Horizontal (Category) Axis Labels); Click Edit and Select D1 to D16, Click Ok

11. Select the Chart and Click Copy

12. Go to Cell J16 and Click Paste

13. Select the 2nd chart

14. Click on Chart Design, Change Chart Type and Choose the Line Chart

15. Select the Bar Chart and Click Chart Design>Add Chart Elements > Data Labels > Outside End

# Lesson 3: Completed

Lesson 3 introduced formulas and graphing basics while reinforcing some of the formatting principles.

| Date | Red | Blue | Green | Yellow | Total Beads |
|------|-----|------|-------|--------|-------------|
| 2/1/2024 | 2 | 2 | 4 | 2 | 10 |
| 2/2/2024 | 4 | 3 | 3 | 4 | 13 |
| 2/3/2024 | 3 | 2 | 3 | 3 | 10 |
| 2/4/2024 | 1 | 3 | 2 | 1 | 8 |
| 2/5/2024 | 3 | 3 | 2 | 2 | 9 |
| 2/6/2024 | 4 | 2 | 3 | 4 | 12 |
| 2/7/2024 | 4 | 3 | 2 | 3 | 11 |
| 2/8/2024 | 3 | 2 | 4 | 2 | 10 |
| 2/9/2024 | 3 | 3 | 3 | 2 | 12 |
| 2/10/2024 | 2 | 3 | 2 | 1 | 8 |
| 2/11/2024 | 2 | 2 | 2 | 2 | 9 |
| 2/12/2024 | 3 | 2 | 1 | 2 | 9 |
| 2/13/2024 | 2 | 1 | 3 | 3 | 9 |
| 2/14/2024 | 4 | 3 | 4 | 2 | 12 |
| 2/15/2024 | 3 | 3 | 5 | 4 | 14 |

Total Beads

Total Beads

# Lesson 3: Practice Sheet

## Filename: 1 Practice Sheet Module 3

## Sheet: Lesson 4 Insert and Draw

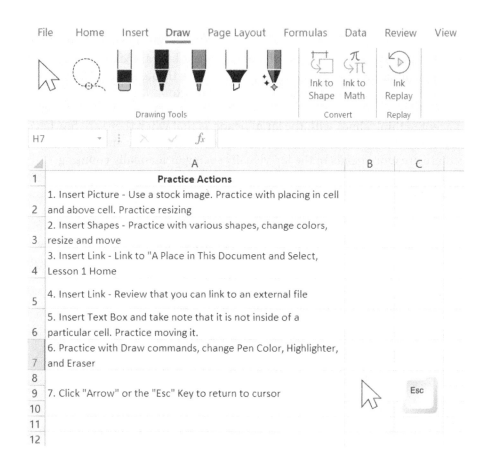

The purpose of Lesson 4 is primarily to raise awareness of the Draw tools. They allow for manually marking, highlighting and writing directly on a sheet. It also shows how to return to a normal cursor or escape from the drawing functionality.

# Summary: Module 4

This module allowed for practice of the different ribbon functionality starting with basic formatting. Manual data entry was highlighted in a lesson and graphs were made using insert charts.

The jar of beads example was introduced as a symbol of one's journey to building their Excel skill set. The jar may be less full initially, and then as skills are learned they can be combined to create different types of solutions. As we work through the course, we will add more beads to the jar, as well as tools in your Excel toolkit!

The other concept to think about with the jar of beads, is that when there are few beads or little data, it is relatively easy to see what is going on with quantity and color. However, as there are more beads in the jar, visually seeing or manually counting becomes more difficult. Data organization and analysis can be used to extract information about a process.

The draw menu was introduced to raise awareness of that functionality. The draw tool set allows for putting shapes and writing over top of cells. Images are also able to be inserted through this menu and there is an option to put it within a cell our over top of cells.

# Module 5

- Page Layout
- Print Set Up

# Lesson 5: Page Layout

The page layout tab is very helpful in getting things formatted and set up for printing. It is a good idea to review the sheet in "File > Print to review a Preview and see how many pages it is creating as a default. With Excel it is very easy to have 100+ pages without realizing it.

For this exercise, a modified version of completed Lesson 3 will be utilized. To start go to the sheet Lesson 5 Page Layout and Click on "File Print" There will be a preview in the center section of the screen.

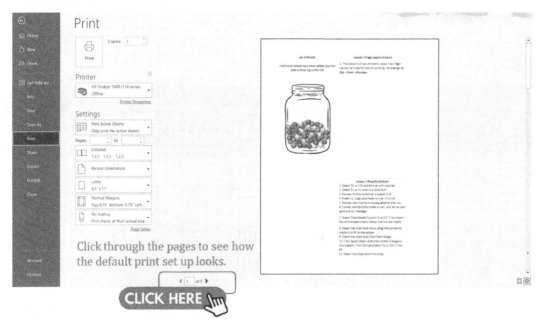

Click through the pages to see how the default print set up looks.

In this example, we can see that we most likely do not want to print with these settings.

# Page Layout (continued)

The printing setup takes practice, let's start by reviewing the settings.

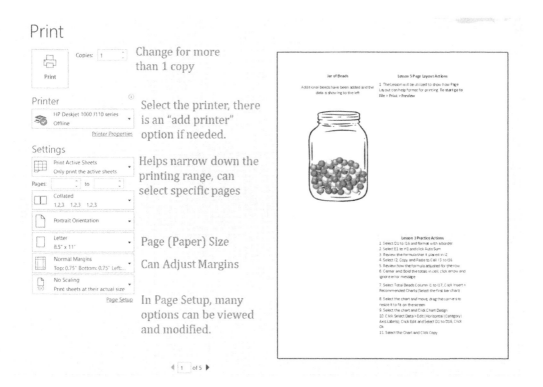

## Print

Copies: 1

**Change for more than 1 copy**

Print

### Printer

HP Deskjet 1000 J110 series
Offline

Printer Properties

**Select the printer, there is an "add printer" option if needed.**

### Settings

Print Active Sheets
Only print the active sheets

Pages: ___ to ___

**Helps narrow down the printing range, can select specific pages**

Collated
1,2,3   1,2,3   1,2,3

Portrait Orientation

Letter
8.5" x 11"

**Page (Paper) Size**

Normal Margins
Top: 0.75" Bottom: 0.75" Left:...

**Can Adjust Margins**

No Scaling
Print sheets at their actual size

Page Setup

**In Page Setup, many options can be viewed and modified.**

◀ 1 of 5 ▶

# Page Layout (continued)

In the View tab, Page Break Preview, allows you to see how the pages are divided with the dotted lines. The dotted lines can be selected and move to adjust the settings. This can be a very effective method and sizing the pages for printing.

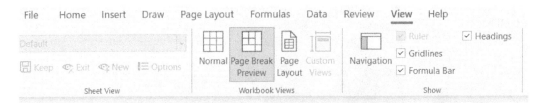

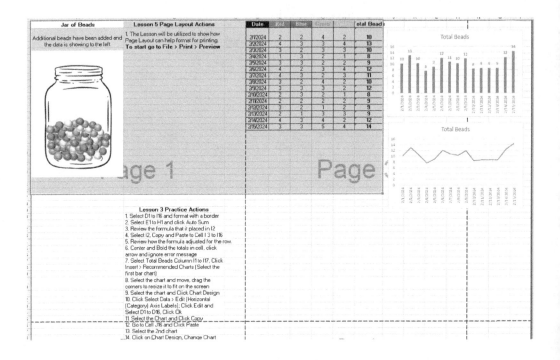

# Page Layout (continued)

Repeating rows at the top of sheet. If you have several pages to your spreadsheet and you want them to all have the same header, "Repeating Rows At the Top" is very helpful. To access it Click Page Layout then the little arrow to expand page set up, Sheet and Rows to Repeat at top. Just select the row(s) desired and preview.

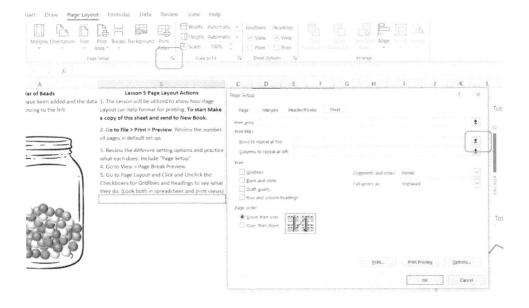

| Order Number | Due Date | Color | Quantity | Last Name | First Name | Address | Email | Phone Number |
|---|---|---|---|---|---|---|---|---|
| 1001 | 12/1/2023 | Blue | 5 | Castillo | Tristin | 142 Arcadia St. New City, NY 10956 | Castillo@email.com | 6399426414 |
| 1002 | 12/10/2023 | Green | 4 | Hayden | Kamari | 15 Whitemarsh St. Sioux Falls, SD 57103 | Hayden@email.com | 6159409984 |
| 1003 | 12/5/2023 | Yellow | 10 | Terry | Maddox | 16 Bear Hill Court Oceanside, NY 11572 | Terry@email.com | 7078224701 |
| 1004 | 12/9/2023 | Blue | 12 | Swanson | Carmen | 203 1st St. Dundalk, MD 21222 | Swanson@email.com | 6434506414 |
| 1005 | 12/8/2023 | Blue | 18 | Bates | Rhys | 21 Manhattan St. Somerset, NJ 08873 | Bates@email.com | 5419860664 |
| 1006 | 12/24/2023 | Blue | 3 | Duncan | Miles | 27 Briarwood Drive Yorktown, VA 23693 | Duncan@email.com | 4773429850 |
| 1007 | 12/30/2023 | Green | 6 | Mcconnell | Shawn | 3 S. Roosevelt St. Council Bluffs, IA 51501 | Mcconnell@email.com | 8552868515 |
| 1008 | 12/18/2023 | Yellow | 12 | Winters | Jazmyn | 357 E. Catherine St. Newton, NJ 07860 | Winters@email.com | 9286895093 |
| 1009 | 12/15/2023 | Red | 15 | Barber | Larissa | 4 Clay Street Bellmore, NY 11710 | Barber@email.com | 9037718958 |
| 1010 | 12/6/2023 | Green | 10 | Jenkins | Sabrina | 4 Glendale Rd. Bridgeport, CT 06606 | Jenkins@email.com | 5953412117 |
| 1011 | 12/15/2023 | Blue | 14 | Weaver | Camille | 470 SE. Corona Street Cockeysville, MD 21030 | Weaver@email.com | 5937510752 |
| 1012 | 12/1/2023 | Yellow | 19 | Ellis | Billy | 549 Kirkland St. El Dorado, AR 71730 | Ellis@email.com | 2159058543 |
| 1013 | 12/10/2023 | Red | 17 | Mccann | Juliana | 62 Honey Creek Lane Pikesville, MD 21208 | Mccann@email.com | 9583612386 |
| 1014 | 12/5/2023 | Red | 8 | Leach | Kaylyn | 7119 Tunnel Court Hattiesburg, MS 39401 | Leach@email.com | 9203649227 |
| 1015 | 12/9/2023 | Red | 5 | Meadows | Eden | 7337 W. San Juan Ave. Beaver Falls, PA 15010 | Meadows@email.com | 7249197939 |
| 1016 | 12/8/2023 | Green | 4 | Mayer | Nigel | 7484 East Hall Drive Prior Lake, MN 55372 | Mayer@email.com | 4064244066 |
| 1017 | 12/24/2023 | Green | 1 | Caldwell | Ellis | 758 Brickyard Court Berwyn, IL 60402 | Caldwell@email.com | 5417305972 |
| 1018 | 12/30/2023 | Green | 12 | Donovan | Meadow | 763 Franklin Lane Elk Grove Village, IL 60007 | Donovan@email.com | 4843126123 |
| 1019 | 12/18/2023 | Yellow | 16 | Floyd | Laney | 7703 Summit Ave. Schenectady, NY 12302 | Floyd@email.com | 5156435785 |
| 1020 | 12/19/2023 | Yellow | 17 | Dixon | Maverick | 8033 Sunbeam Drive Summerville, SC 29483 | Dixon@email.com | 7964472039 |
| 1021 | 12/1/2023 | Green | 12 | Anderson | Steve | 1 High Noon St. Adrian, MI 49221 | Anderson@email.com | 4047594303 |
| 1022 | 12/10/2023 | Yellow | 14 | Williamson | Zack | 114 North Bedford Street Chicago Heights, IL 60411 | Williamson@email.com | 4423504364 |

| Order Numb | Due Date | Color | Quantity | Last Name | First Name | Address | Email | Phone Number |
|---|---|---|---|---|---|---|---|---|
| 1001 | 12/1/2023 | Blue | 5 | Castillo | Tristin | 142 Arcadia St. New City, NY 10956 | Castillo@email.com | 6399426414 |
| 1002 | 12/10/2023 | Green | 4 | Hayden | Kamari | 15 Whitemarsh St. Sioux Falls, SD 57103 | Hayden@email.com | 6159409984 |
| 1003 | 12/5/2023 | Yellow | 10 | Terry | Maddox | 16 Bear Hill Court Oceanside, NY 11572 | Terry@email.com | 7078224701 |
| 1004 | 12/9/2023 | Blue | 12 | Swanson | Carmen | 203 1st St. Dundalk, MD 21222 | Swanson@email.com | 6434506414 |
| 1005 | 12/8/2023 | Blue | 18 | Bates | Rhys | 21 Manhattan St. Somerset, NJ 08873 | Bates@email.com | 5419860664 |
| 1006 | ####### | Blue | 3 | Duncan | Miles | 27 Briarwood Drive Yorktown, VA 23693 | Duncan@email.com | 4773429850 |
| 1007 | ####### | Green | 6 | Mcconnell | Shawn | 3 S. Roosevelt St. Council Bluffs, IA 51501 | Mcconnell@email.co | 8552868515 |
| 1008 | 12/18/2023 | Yellow | 12 | Winters | Jazmyn | 357 E. Catherine St. Newton, NJ 07860 | Winters@email.com | 9286895093 |
| 1009 | 12/15/2023 | Red | 15 | Barber | Larissa | 4 Clay Street Bellmore, NY 11710 | Barber@email.com | 9037718958 |
| 1010 | 12/6/2023 | Green | 10 | Jenkins | Sabrina | 4 Glendale Rd. Bridgeport, CT 06606 | Jenkins@email.com | 5953412117 |
| 1011 | 12/15/2023 | Blue | 14 | Weaver | Camille | 470 SE. Corona Street Cockeysville, MD 21030 | Weaver@email.com | 5937510752 |
| 1012 | 12/1/2023 | Yellow | 19 | Ellis | Billy | 549 Kirkland St. El Dorado, AR 71730 | Ellis@email.com | 2159058543 |
| 1013 | 12/10/2023 | Red | 17 | Mccann | Juliana | 62 Honey Creek Lane Pikesville, MD 21208 | Mccann@email.com | 9583612386 |
| 1014 | 12/5/2023 | Red | 8 | Leach | Kaylyn | 7119 Tunnel Court Hattiesburg, MS 39401 | Leach@email.com | 9203649227 |
| 1015 | 12/9/2023 | Red | 5 | Meadows | Eden | 7337 W. San Juan Ave. Beaver Falls, PA 15010 | Meadows@email.co | 7249197939 |
| 1016 | 12/8/2023 | Green | 4 | Mayer | Nigel | 7484 East Hall Drive Prior Lake, MN 55372 | Mayer@email.com | 4064244066 |
| 1017 | ####### | Green | 1 | Caldwell | Ellis | 758 Brickyard Court Berwyn, IL 60402 | Caldwell@email.com | 5417305972 |
| 1018 | ####### | Green | 12 | Donovan | Meadow | 763 Franklin Lane Elk Grove Village, IL 60007 | Donovan@email.cor | 4843126123 |
| 1019 | 12/18/2023 | Yellow | 16 | Floyd | Laney | 7703 Summit Ave. Schenectady, NY 12302 | Floyd@email.com | 5156435785 |
| 1020 | 12/19/2023 | Yellow | 17 | Dixon | Maverick | 8033 Sunbeam Drive Summerville, SC 29483 | Dixon@email.com | 7964472039 |
| 1021 | 12/1/2023 | Green | 12 | Anderson | Steve | 1 High Noon St. Adrian, MI 49221 | Anderson@email.com | 4047594303 |
| 1022 | 12/10/2023 | Yellow | 14 | Williamson | Zack | 114 North Bedford Street Chicago Heights, IL 60411 | Williamson@email.cc | 4423504364 |
| 1023 | 12/5/2023 | Red | 16 | Estrada | Celia | 12 Longfellow St. Selden, NY 11784 | Estrada@email.com | 8272142095 |
| 1024 | 12/9/2023 | Green | 2 | Stanley | Ellie | 13 Trenton Ave. Norristown, PA 19401 | Stanley@email.com | 3612150239 |
| 1025 | 12/8/2023 | Blue | 5 | Parrish | Royce | 199 S. Penn Court Rockville Centre, NY 11570 | Parrish@email.com | 5226133609 |
| 1026 | ####### | Yellow | 8 | Adkins | Emilio | 1C Princeton Dr. Strongsville, OH 44136 | Adkins@email.com | 2126886798 |
| 1027 | ####### | Red | 7 | Wilcox | Nathan | 2 Kent St. Evanston, IL 60201 | Wilcox@email.com | 3956706442 |
| 1028 | 12/18/2023 | Red | 15 | Mcgee | Shamar | 2 Saxton St. Rockledge, FL 32955 | Mcgee@email.com | 9179369087 |
| 1029 | 12/15/2023 | Red | 16 | Huynh | Nathanial | 236 Hudson St. Jeffersonville, IN 47130 | Huynh@email.com | 7276265060 |
| 1030 | 12/6/2023 | Green | 6 | Mathis | Kaiya | 243 Bayport Ave. Easton, PA 18042 | Mathis@email.com | 9114449237 |
| 1031 | 12/15/2023 | Yellow | 4 | Weber | Yurem | 35 Theatre Street Grandville, MI 49418 | Weber@email.com | 7686192338 |
| 1032 | 12/1/2023 | Red | 12 | Bartlett | Chance | 36 Oklahoma St. Crofton, MD 21114 | Bartlett@email.com | 2192962968 |
| 1033 | 12/10/2023 | Green | 3 | Barnett | Raven | 436 Leatherwood Street Wausau, WI 54401 | Barnett@email.com | 5542957239 |
| 1034 | 12/5/2023 | Blue | 19 | Sullivan | Brodie | 5 Stonybrook Ave. Westlake, OH 44145 | Sullivan@email.com | 5138196569 |
| 1035 | 12/9/2023 | Yellow | 20 | Cruz | Isiah | 53 East Creek Lane Sun City, AZ 85351 | Cruz@email.com | 5507417306 |
| 1036 | 12/8/2023 | Red | 7 | Zamora | Pamela | 602 Lyme St. Central Islip, NY 11722 | Zamora@email.com | 8183921517 |
| 1037 | ####### | Red | 18 | Leon | Kennedy | 606 N. Buttonwood Lane South Richmond Hill, NY | Leon@email.com | 2607079515 |
| 1038 | ####### | Red | 4 | Anthony | Sanaa | 7040 Linden St. Johnston, RI 02919 | Anthony@email.com | 5667619033 |
| 1039 | 12/18/2023 | Green | 6 | Bradley | Kamari | 709 Prospect Ave. Sarasota, FL 34231 | Bradley@email.com | 4866173469 |
| 1040 | 12/19/2023 | Yellow | 5 | Bender | Sonia | 7204 Galvin Rd. Fitchburg, MA 01420 | Bender@email.com | 3765197271 |
| 1041 | 12/9/2023 | Red | 2 | Shaffer | Lexie | 7344 Applegate Avenue Southampton, PA 18966 | Shaffer@email.com | 5948159574 |
| 1042 | 12/8/2023 | Green | 8 | Esparza | Haiden | 7425 Chestnut Drive Mason, OH 45040 | Esparza@email.co | 4144529488 |
| 1043 | ####### | Blue | 9 | Wheeler | Leonidas | 816 Ann Street Miamisburg, OH 45342 | Wheeler@email.com | 8938003820 |
| 1044 | ####### | Yellow | 4 | Johnson | Leonardo | 855 Glen Creek St. Lititz, PA 17543 | Johnson@email.com | 4175100487 |
| 1045 | 12/18/2023 | Red | 12 | Howell | Arnav | 8707 Fordham Street Fort Washington, MD 20744 | Howell@email.com | 5773905511 |
| 1046 | 12/19/2023 | Red | 14 | Peck | Trinity | 88 North Pierce Road Faribault, MN 55021 | Peck@email.com | 5306625827 |
| 1047 | 12/9/2023 | Red | 11 | Huang | Jude | 8858 Hall Ave. Urbandale, IA 50322 | Huang@email.com | 8616980549 |
| 1048 | 12/8/2023 | Green | 10 | Mendez | Holly | 8867 W. Rosewood St. Green Cove Springs, FL 320 | Mendez@email.com | 3384251499 |
| 1049 | ####### | Blue | 18 | Heath | Keyon | 8869 Winchester Ave. Hialeah, FL 33010 | Heath@email.com | 5748522917 |
| 1050 | ####### | Yellow | 17 | Smith | Jorge | 979 Race Street Suitland, MD 20746 | Smith@email.com | 5715362391 |

Practice: Rows to Repeat at Top: Page Layout, Expand Small Area, Page Set Up, Sheet, Rows to Repeat at Top. Click Preview & Scroll to see the result.

Module 5

Practice: For Print Setup – go to Print and Page Set Up – Change orientation to Landscape and Fit to 1 wide by 1 tall. In Margins – set on "Center on Page" Check Horizontally and Vertically.

End Result of Landscape and Centered

Practice: Select Cell B2. Go to View > Freeze Panes > Select the 1st Option

# Summary: Module 5

There are times when spreadsheets will be printed. The File > Print option shows a preview of what each page looks like and how many there are. It is very easy to unintentionally have many pages. These tools help to understand and manage the layout and adjust accordingly. The Page Setup option allows for easy switching between portrait and landscape layout. It also has a feature where the number of pages wide and tall can be select and Excel will auto fit to that set up.

The View > Page Break View will show dotted lines and indicate how many pages there are and where the page breaks exist. From this menu it is possible to move the page breaks by selecting and moving the dotted lines.

For longer spreadsheets the header rows can be added to the top of each page by selecting the Page Layout tab and clicking the small little arrow in the bottom right corner. This opens up a menu where sheet can be selected and rows to repeat at top is selected. Choose the row or rows that contain the header values to show on each printed page. Within this menu is also where page size can be changed, as well as margins. There is a center feature within margins where the result can be centered horizontally and vertically for printing.

Page layout can also be used with the Print Area option to select parts of the sheet and selecting print area. This will only show the selected rows for printing. The result can be viewed in the Print Preview.

# Module 6

- Working with Data Sets: Marketing Data
  - Bar Graph
  - Formatting Charts
  - If Statements
  - Conditional Formatting
  - Visual Indicators with Tables
  - Multiply and Divide Formulas
  - Gridlines vs No Gridlines on Spreadsheet

# Module 6 Moving Forward

Prior Modules served as an overview of the general layout of a spreadsheet and looked within the ribbon, different menu buttons, tabs and commands.

As we work though practice examples and build upon a foundation, application of these features will be put into action.

- Data Collection
- Data Organization
- Data Analysis

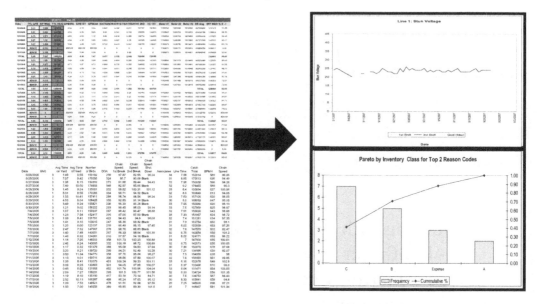

# Module 6: Working with Data Sets

In this example, we will use an example Marketing Dataset. The data consists of Leads per Month and Lead Sources. Conditional Formatting and Wingding shapes will be utilized. Various Chart examples will be made, and built-in formatting options will be reviewed.

| Month | Leads | Goal | Meet Goal |
|-------|-------|------|-----------|
| Jan | 100 | 150 | |
| Feb | 125 | 150 | |
| Mar | 118 | 150 | |
| Apr | 130 | 150 | |
| May | 132 | 150 | |
| Jun | 140 | 150 | |
| Jul | 150 | 150 | |
| Aug | 145 | 150 | |
| Sep | 160 | 150 | |
| Oct | | 150 | |
| Nov | | 150 | |
| Dec | | 150 | |

| Month | Leads | Goal | Meet Goal | Smile? | Difference Month to Month |
|-------|-------|------|-----------|--------|---------------------------|
| Jan | 100 | 150 | No | ☹ | |
| Feb | 125 | 150 | No | ☹ | ⬆ 25 |
| Mar | 118 | 150 | No | ☹ | ⬇ 7 |
| Apr | 130 | 150 | No | ☹ | ⬆ 12 |
| May | 132 | 150 | No | ☹ | ⬆ 2 |
| Jun | 140 | 150 | No | ☹ | ⬆ 8 |
| Jul | 150 | 150 | Yes | ☺ | ⬆ 10 |
| Aug | 145 | 150 | No | ☹ | ⬇ 5 |
| Sep | 160 | 150 | Yes | ☺ | ⬆ 15 |
| Oct | | 150 | No | ☹ | |
| Nov | | 150 | No | ☹ | |
| Dec | | 150 | No | ☹ | |

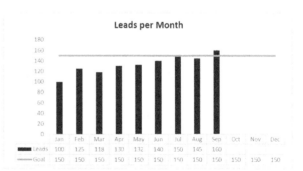

**Leads per Month**

| | Jan | Feb | Mar | Apr | May | Jun | Jul | Aug | Sep | Oct | Nov | Dec |
|------|-----|-----|-----|-----|-----|-----|-----|-----|-----|-----|-----|-----|
| Leads | 100 | 125 | 118 | 130 | 132 | 140 | 150 | 145 | 160 | | | |
| Goal | 150 | 150 | 150 | 150 | 150 | 150 | 150 | 150 | 150 | 150 | 150 | 150 |

Highlight the Month through Goal (A1 to C13)

| Month | Leads | Goal | Meet Goal |
|-------|-------|------|-----------|
| Jan | 100 | 150 | |
| Feb | 125 | 150 | |
| Mar | 118 | 150 | |
| Apr | 130 | 150 | |
| May | 132 | 150 | |
| Jun | 140 | 150 | |
| Jul | 150 | 150 | |
| Aug | 145 | 150 | |
| Sep | 160 | 150 | |
| Oct | | 150 | |
| Nov | | 150 | |
| Dec | | 150 | |

# Insert > Recommended Charts > Clustered Column > Ok

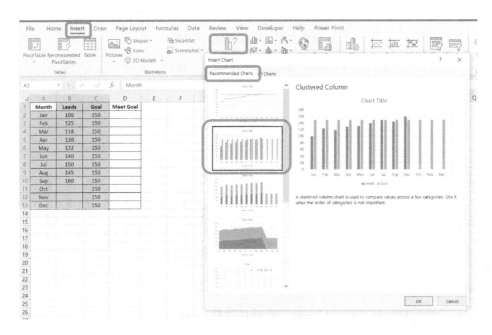

The result is a basic bar chart with 2 bars per each month, one for leads and one for the goal.

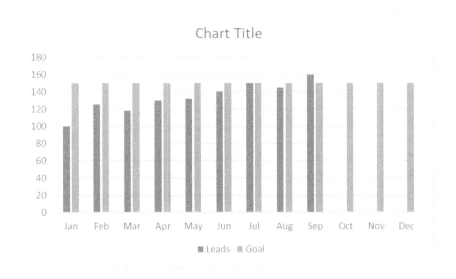

Select the Vertical Axis Gridlines – click on 1 of them and they will all become selected.

Press the "Delete" Button. This will remove the gridlines. This is personal preference, so if they are desired, just click "Undo"

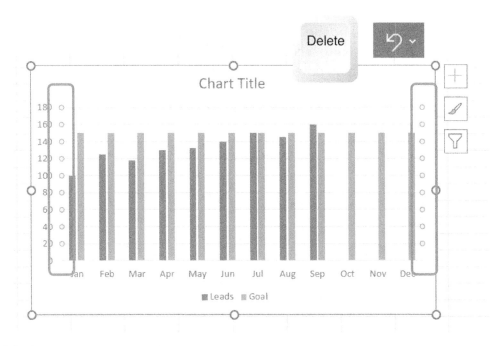

Click inside the Title "Chart" and backspace then enter the title "Leads per Month"

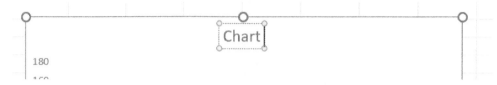

The formatting toolbars can be used to change the font to Black and Bold

The next step will be the formatting of the bars. The graph is going to be changed to a combination line chart for the goal line and a bar for the lead data. The bar will be changed to black and the goal line green. These steps are usually not difficult, it is just a matter of getting used to where to click and select. Sometimes the details are subtle.

Select just the orange "goal line" bar. Clicking on 1, will select them all. After the goal bars are selected, Click Chart Design > Change Chart Type. Notice that it brings up a panel where the type of chart by data series can be selected. In this case, we have 2 series: Leads and Goal.

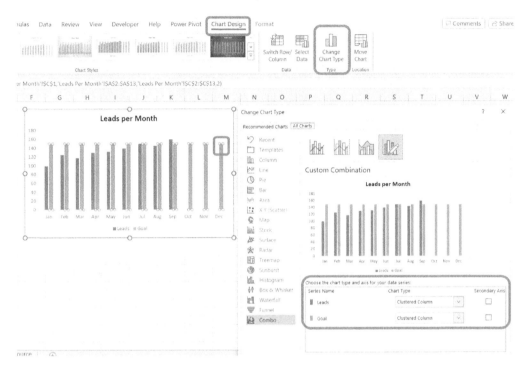

For reference, the Change Chart Design feature can be used to switch between chart types. It is a good practice to click on different ones to view the data in different ways. For this example, change the goal to a line, as shown below.

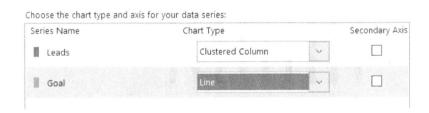

This is a combination line / bar chart. The next steps will be to change the colors of the bar and the line. Then data labels will be added.

To change the color of the bar, select one of the bars by clicking 1 time and it will select all of them. Each should have the "2 little circles"

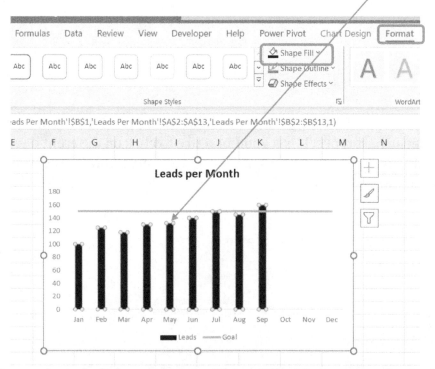

Once selected, click on Format > Shape Fill and change to the desired color. In this case, the bars are changed to black.

Repeat similar steps to change the line to green. Select the line, as shown below. Then go to Format > Shape Outline and change to green.

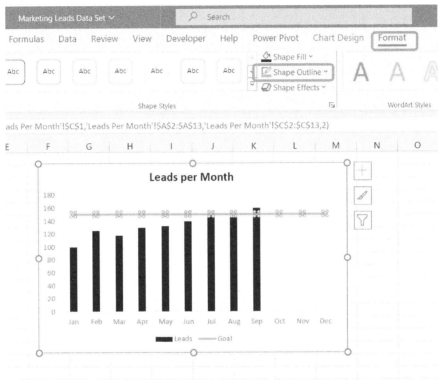

The result is shown below.

Data labels will be added to each of the bars in order to display the actual number of leads corresponding to that bar.  A Data Table underneath the graph will also be shown.

Select the bars by clicking one time on 1 bar. This will select them all.  Then go to Chart Design > Add Chart Element > Data Labels > Outside End.  You can experiment with different locations for data labels.

## The result is shown below.

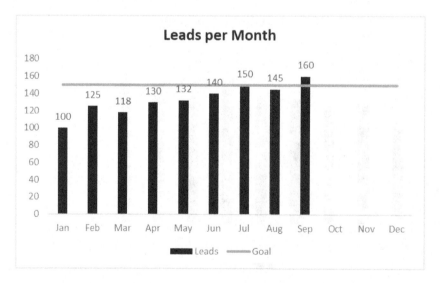

Another look for displaying the numeric information is shown below. This is called a "Data Table with Legend Keys". This is added in the same menu as data labels by selecting Data Table instead of Data Labels. In this example, the data labels and legend were removed after adding the data table.

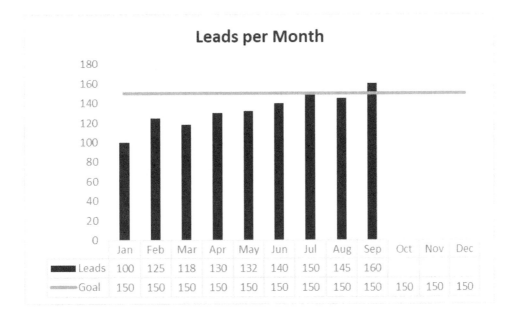

The legend and data labels can be removed either by clicking on them and pressing the delete button or going into Chart Design > Add Chart Element and change their respective selections to "none".

As with many of the commands and functions within Excel, there are multiple ways to perform a given step. Practice is the best way to determine your own personal best techniques.

This exercise will continue working back with the data table. If statements will be used to determine if the leads meet the goal per month. Conditional formatting will be added, as well as some simple visual indicators using different fonts and icon sets.

In writing an "If" statement, the formula will start out like other formula operations, with an = sign indicating that there is an operation to follow. Start by typing =if( in the cell and it can be noticed that some helper information shows up, showing the general format of the formula.  It can be helpful to being getting used to those as they can be helpful guides and serve as reminders moving forward.

The format for this type of If statement is If "what" is true, then what, if not, then what. With formulas to operate correctly, the details of , and ) positioning is critical.  That is where the guides come in handy!

If we were going to write this out in a sentence, it would be something like….If the Leads are greater than or equal to the goal then "Yes" if not then "No". The formula behaves in a similar way.  Another note, in this example we will use text values of Yes and No where in other cases we may use a numeric value like 1 or 0 if the intention is to perform additional mathematical operations.  When writing any type of text in a formula it must be enclosed in " ". This is the indicator to Excel that it is text vs a value.

The completed formula can be seen highlighted in the formula bar below. Take note of the use of cell references. This will allow the formula to move appropriately when it is copied down to the remaining cells.

To copy it down, the Copy and Paste icon can be used or the auto fill click by a quick double click in the bottom right corner of the cell.

| D2 | | | | $f_x$ | =IF(B2>=C2,"Yes","No") | |
|----|----|----|----|----|----|----|
| | A | B | C | D | E | F |
| 1 | Month | Leads | Goal | Meet Goal | Smile? | Difference Month to Month |
| 2 | Jan | 100 | 150 | No | | |
| 3 | Feb | 125 | 150 | No | | |
| 4 | Mar | 118 | 150 | No | | |
| 5 | Apr | 130 | 150 | No | | |
| 6 | May | 132 | 150 | No | | |
| 7 | Jun | 140 | 150 | No | | |
| 8 | Jul | 150 | 150 | Yes | | |
| 9 | Aug | 145 | 150 | No | | |
| 10 | Sep | 160 | 150 | Yes | | |
| 11 | Oct | | 150 | No | | |
| 12 | Nov | | 150 | No | | |
| 13 | Dec | | 150 | No | | |
| 14 | | | | | | |

After copying this formula down, we can see that it moved to each row.

Conditional formatting will be added to the Yes and No with the indication that Yes is Green and No is Red.

Highlight the cells containing the Yes's and No's, then click Home >
Conditional Formatting > New Rule

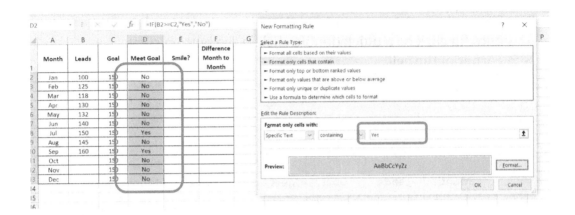

The option Format Only Cells that contain is chosen and since we
are using text, the option specific text was select. Yes was entered
and a light green color is selected.

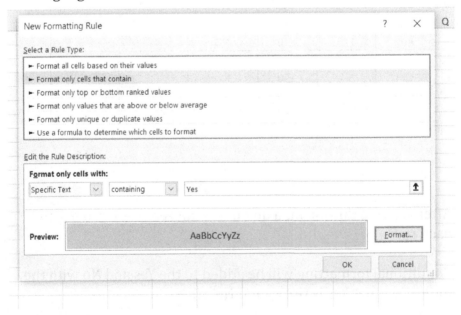

This step is repeated for the No and making it a red color.

The Yes and No along with color will automatically change based on the value in the leads column. This can be tested by entering different values in the leads column. Try it with some above and some below and see what it does if it is exactly the value.

| Month | Leads | Goal | Meet Goal |
|-------|-------|------|-----------|
| Jan | 100 | 150 | No |
| Feb | 125 | 150 | No |
| Mar | 118 | 150 | No |
| Apr | 130 | 150 | No |
| May | 132 | 150 | No |
| Jun | 140 | 150 | No |
| Jul | 150 | 150 | Yes |
| Aug | 145 | 150 | No |
| Sep | 160 | 150 | Yes |
| Oct | | 150 | No |
| Nov | | 150 | No |
| Dec | | 150 | No |

Since the Yes is the result if it is greater than or +, the Yes and Green will appear when the value is exact. This is triggered by putting the equal sign in the formula when we wrote the if statement.

Conditional formatting is a "format"; therefore, the Format Painter operation will work to transfer the conditional formatting to other cells. This can be a time saver!

    Format Painter

It is worth taking a look within the menu options of conditional formatting to see some of the various features available.

The steps below, will allow for clearing the formatting from a cell or the entire sheet. Always remember if a mistake is made, the un-do button can be hit that will take back to the last save.

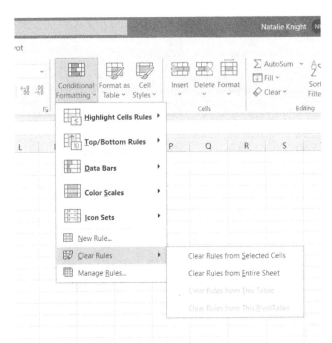

The manage rule options is commonly used to review the formatting. It shows the cells it applies to, logic and order. The rule will follow in order and will end with the last condition on the list so sometimes it is necessary to check the box "stop if true".

A combination of techniques will be utilized to add a visual smiley face or sad face depending on whether on not goal is met. There is a font within Microsoft call "Wingdings" and different letters and numbers actual represent a symbol in this font. An internet search can help provide the font and symbol combinations. An upper-case J is a smile, and an upper-case L is a frown. The if statement off of the yes or no field will return either the J or the L. Then the font is changed to Wingding in format tab and the results are as shown below.

| Clipboard | | ⌐ | | Font | | ⌐ |

| E2 | | ⋮ | × | ✓ | $f_x$ | =IF(D2="Yes","J","L") |

| | A | B | C | D | E | F |
|---|---|---|---|---|---|---|
| 1 | Month | Leads | Goal | Meet Goal | Smile? | Difference Month to Month |
| 2 | Jan | 100 | 150 | No | ☹ | |
| 3 | Feb | 125 | 150 | No | ☹ | |
| 4 | Mar | 118 | 150 | No | ☹ | |

The If statement formula is highlighted in the formula bar. The Windings font selection can be seen. Once complete the formula and formatting is copied down.

| Month | Leads | Goal | Meet Goal | Smile? |
|---|---|---|---|---|
| Jan | 100 | 150 | No | ☹ |
| Feb | 125 | 150 | No | ☹ |
| Mar | 118 | 150 | No | ☹ |
| Apr | 130 | 150 | No | ☹ |
| May | 132 | 150 | No | ☹ |
| Jun | 140 | 150 | No | ☹ |
| Jul | 150 | 150 | Yes | ☺ |
| Aug | 145 | 150 | No | ☹ |
| Sep | 160 | 150 | Yes | ☺ |
| Oct | | 150 | No | ☹ |
| Nov | | 150 | No | ☹ |
| Dec | | 150 | No | ☹ |

The last example of this section will be related to looking at differences month to month and using an Icon set within the cell to indicate the direction. A formula will be created to calculate the difference and will need to be modified to account for months with no data yet.

The result is shown below.

| Month | Leads | Goal | Meet Goal | Smile? | Difference Month to Month |
|-------|-------|------|-----------|--------|---------------------------|
| Jan | 100 | 150 | No | ☹ | |
| Feb | 125 | 150 | No | ☹ | ⬆ 25 |
| Mar | 118 | 150 | No | ☹ | ⬇ -7 |
| Apr | 130 | 150 | No | ☹ | ⬆ 12 |
| May | 132 | 150 | No | ☹ | ⬆ 2 |
| Jun | 140 | 150 | No | ☹ | ⬆ 8 |
| Jul | 150 | 150 | Yes | ☺ | ⬆ 10 |
| Aug | 145 | 150 | No | ☹ | ⬇ -5 |
| Sep | 160 | 150 | Yes | ☺ | ⬆ 15 |
| Oct | | 150 | No | ☹ | |
| Nov | | 150 | No | ☹ | |
| Dec | | 150 | No | ☹ | |

This exercise starts with a simple formula taking the difference from the row and the prior row. Starting with the February month the formula is B3-B2 resulting in the 125-100 = 25. Copy this formula to all cells.

| F3 | | | $f_x$ | =B3-B2 | | |
|----|---|---|-------|--------|---|---|
| | A | B | C | D | E | F |
| 1 | Month | Leads | Goal | Meet Goal | Smile? | Difference Month to Month |
| 2 | Jan | 100 | 150 | No | ☹ | |
| 3 | Feb | 125 | 150 | No | ☹ | 25 |
| 4 | Mar | 118 | 150 | No | ☹ | |

A problem can be seen starting in October. Because there is no value in October, the difference became 160 and then there is no difference showing between Dec and Nov. The original formula will be modified to account for a blank cell. It is basically going to say if the cell for leads in blank than return a blank. The operator for a blanks is "" and is very communing used in formulas.

| Month | Leads | Goal | Meet Goal | Smile? | Difference Month to Month |
|-------|-------|------|-----------|--------|---------------------------|
| Jan | 100 | 150 | No | ☹ | |
| Feb | 125 | 150 | No | ☹ | 25 |
| Mar | 118 | 150 | No | ☹ | -7 |
| Apr | 130 | 150 | No | ☹ | 12 |
| May | 132 | 150 | No | ☹ | 2 |
| Jun | 140 | 150 | No | ☹ | 8 |
| Jul | 150 | 150 | Yes | ☺ | 10 |
| Aug | 145 | 150 | No | ☹ | -5 |
| Sep | 160 | 150 | Yes | ☺ | 15 |
| Oct | | 150 | No | ☹ | -160 |
| Nov | | 150 | No | ☹ | 0 |
| Dec | | 150 | No | ☹ | 0 |

The formula modification is shown below along with the desired result.

| F3 | | | | fx | =IF(B3="","",B3-B2) | |
|----|---|---|---|----|----|----|

| | A | B | C | D | E | F |
|---|---|---|---|---|---|---|
| | Jan | 100 | 150 | No | ☹ | Difference Month to Month |
| 1 | Feb | 125 | 150 | No | ☹ | |
| 2 | Mar | 118 | 150 | No | ☹ | |
| 3 | Apr | 130 | 150 | No | ☹ | 25 |
| 4 | May | 132 | 150 | No | ☹ | -7 |
| 5 | | | | | | 12 |
| 6 | Jun | 140 | 150 | No | ☹ | 2 |
| 7 | Jul | 150 | 150 | Yes | ☺ | 8 |
| 8 | Aug | 145 | 150 | No | ☹ | 10 |
| 9 | Sep | 160 | 150 | Yes | ☺ | -5 |
| 10 | | | | | | 15 |
| 11 | Oct | | 150 | No | ☹ | |
| 12 | Nov | | 150 | No | ☹ | |
| 13 | Dec | | 150 | No | ☹ | |
| 14 | | | | | | |

To reach the Icon Set Menu – go to Conditional Formatting > Icon Sets > Directional and choose the first option.

Enter Conditional Formatting > Manage Rules > Edit Rule and enter the settings below.

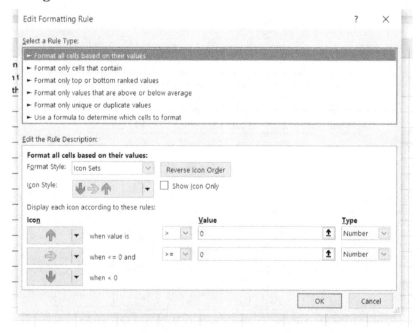

# Summary

| Month | Leads | Goal |
|-------|-------|------|
| Jan | 100 | 150 |
| Feb | 125 | 150 |
| Mar | 118 | 150 |
| Apr | 130 | 150 |
| May | 132 | 150 |
| Jun | 140 | 150 |
| Jul | 150 | 150 |
| Aug | 145 | 150 |
| Sep | 160 | 150 |
| Oct | | 150 |
| Nov | | 150 |
| Dec | | 150 |

In this section, the simple table on the left was transformed into a table with visual indicators as well as a combination line and bar graph. Formulas, If Statements and conditional formatting was utilized.

| Month | Leads | Goal | Meet Goal | Smile? | Difference Month to Month |
|-------|-------|------|-----------|--------|---------------------------|
| Jan | 100 | 150 | No | ☹ | |
| Feb | 125 | 150 | No | ☹ | ⬆ 25 |
| Mar | 118 | 150 | No | ☹ | ⬇ -7 |
| Apr | 130 | 150 | No | ☹ | ⬆ 12 |
| May | 132 | 150 | No | ☹ | ⬆ 2 |
| Jun | 140 | 150 | No | ☹ | ⬆ 8 |
| Jul | 150 | 150 | Yes | ☺ | ⬆ 10 |
| Aug | 145 | 150 | No | ☹ | ⬇ -5 |
| Sep | 160 | 150 | Yes | ☺ | ⬆ 15 |
| Oct | | 150 | No | ☹ | |
| Nov | | 150 | No | ☹ | |
| Dec | | 150 | No | ☹ | |

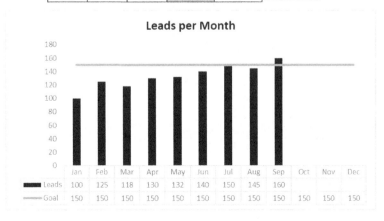

**Leads per Month**

| | Jan | Feb | Mar | Apr | May | Jun | Jul | Aug | Sep | Oct | Nov | Dec |
|------|-----|-----|-----|-----|-----|-----|-----|-----|-----|-----|-----|-----|
| Leads | 100 | 125 | 118 | 130 | 132 | 140 | 150 | 145 | 160 | | | |
| Goal | 150 | 150 | 150 | 150 | 150 | 150 | 150 | 150 | 150 | 150 | 150 | 150 |

Transitioning to another aspect of a marketing example, leads generated by lead source will be analyzed. Formulas will be used to calculation conversion rate, $ spent on leads and Revenue $ generated. For this example, use an average cost per lead of $100 and average revenue from a converted lead of $2500.

| Marketing Source | Leads | Converted Leads | Conv. Rate | $ Spent on Leads | $ Revenue Generated |
|---|---|---|---|---|---|
| Website | 13 | 12 | | | |
| Social Media | 107 | 19 | | | |
| Sale Flyer | 20 | 15 | | | |
| Referral Program | 12 | 10 | | | |
| Email Special | 55 | 32 | | | |

## Conversion Rate Formula: Number of Converted Leads / Leads

D2     $f_x$   =C2/B2

| | A | B | C | D | E | F |
|---|---|---|---|---|---|---|
| 1 | Marketing Source | Leads | Converted Leads | Conv. Rate | $ Spent on Leads | $ Revenue Generated |
| 2 | Website | 13 | 12 | 92% | | |
| 3 | Social Media | 107 | 19 | 18% | | |
| 4 | Sale Flyer | 20 | 15 | 75% | | |
| 5 | Referral Program | 12 | 10 | 83% | | |
| 6 | Email Special | 55 | 32 | 58% | | |
| 7 | | | | | | |

The $ per lead formula is shown below and the $ revenue is the same except replacing the 100 with 2500. Columns E and F are formatted as $.

E2     $f_x$   =B2*100

| | A | B | C | D | E | F |
|---|---|---|---|---|---|---|
| 1 | Marketing Source | Leads | Converted Leads | Conv. Rate | $ Spent on Leads | $ Revenue Generated |
| 2 | Website | 13 | 12 | 92% | $ 1,300 | $ 30,000 |
| 3 | Social Media | 107 | 19 | 18% | $ 10,700 | $ 47,500 |
| 4 | Sale Flyer | 20 | 15 | 75% | $ 2,000 | $ 37,500 |
| 5 | Referral Program | 12 | 10 | 83% | $ 1,200 | $ 25,000 |
| 6 | Email Special | 55 | 32 | 58% | $ 5,500 | $ 80,000 |

For this table, conditional formatting, the built in color scales will be used. Highlight the cells with the conversion rate numbers and go to Conditional Formatting > Color Scales > and choose the top left option.

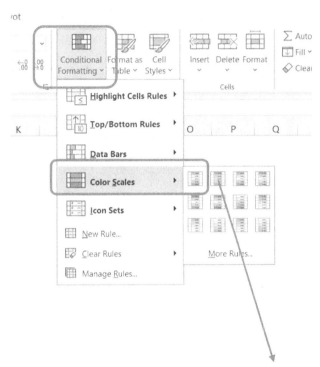

| Marketing Source | Leads | Converted Leads | Conv. Rate | $ Spent on Leads | $ Revenue Generated |
|---|---|---|---|---|---|
| Website | 13 | 12 | 92% | $ 1,300 | $ 30,000 |
| Social Media | 107 | 19 | 18% | $ 10,700 | $ 47,500 |
| Sale Flyer | 20 | 15 | 75% | $ 2,000 | $ 37,500 |
| Referral Program | 12 | 10 | 83% | $ 1,200 | $ 25,000 |
| Email Special | 55 | 32 | 58% | $ 5,500 | $ 80,000 |

Do this formatting for each of the 3 columns as shown. The only difference is that since a lower cost spent on leads is better the 2nd option was selected as it reverses the colors have the highest number red where in the other 2 cases the higher number is green.

This relative scales are great for visually comparing numbers in a table. We can quickly see that the most revenue generated was from the Email Special and we spent the most $ on Social Media.

Sort the data from high to low based on the number of leads using the Data Sort Z to A feature.

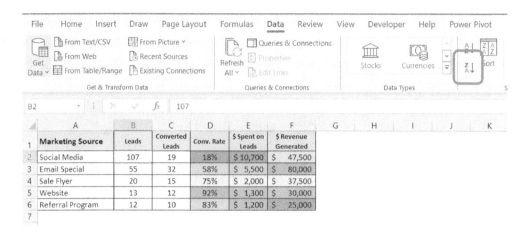

Select the data in the first 2 columns and choose Insert > Bar Chart

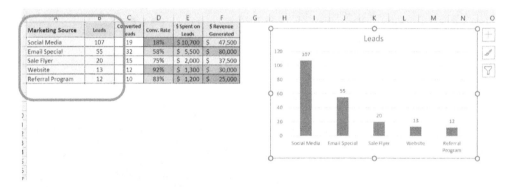

In Chart Design – Practice scrolling through the different color schemes and format options.

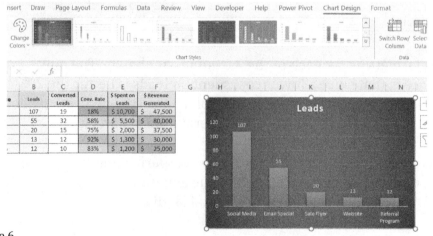

Create a copy of the chart by selecting it and clicking copy. Go to another cell in this case a cell below the chart was selected. Then click paste. A duplicate of the chart was created.

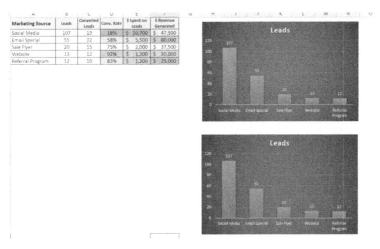

With the bottom chart selected, grab the outline around leads and drag it over to converted leads. This will change the data source to converted leads and create the 2nd graph below.

| Marketing Source | Leads | Converted Leads |
|---|---|---|
| Social Media | 107 | 19 |
| Email Special | 55 | 32 |
| Sale Flyer | 20 | 15 |
| Website | 13 | 12 |
| Referral Program | 12 | 10 |

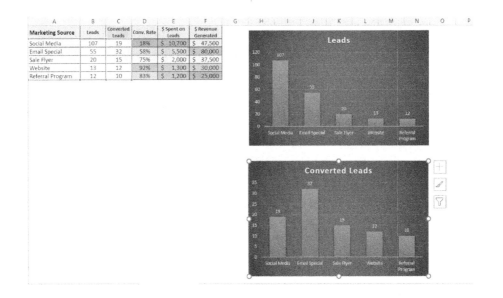

## Chart Creation

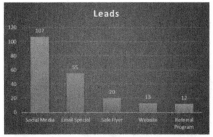

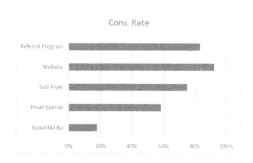

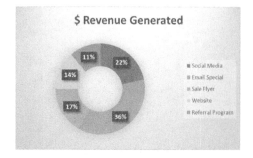

The copy and change source data steps were repeated. To generate different chart types, click Chart Design > Change Chart Type. There are different examples shown. The color of the fill in the bar or pie chart can be changed by clicking on it and formatting the fill to a different color.

Often when display graphs for summary information, users will remove the gridlines by unchecking the gridlines checkbox.

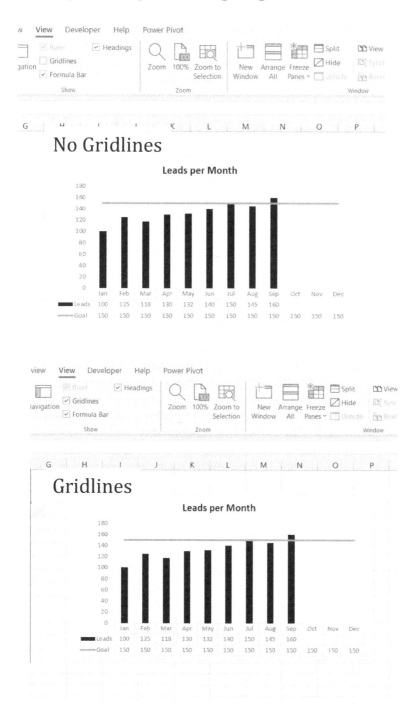

# Summary: Module 6

We reviewed that Microsoft Excel is for storing, organizing and analyzing data. It can be helpful to breakdown the processes of Data Entry, Organization and Storage separately. When considering how the data is being acquired, this affects the set up of the sheet. If it is a manual data entry process, then streamlining for the user would be a priority. Techniques to improve flow and reduce keystrokes are helpful. Drop down menus and formulas are some examples. If data is coming from a system or another spreadsheet, methods to facilitate the merging the data sets together. No matter what method, data accuracy should always be a top priority.

The optimization of data organization can allow for greater flexibly to meet the needs and preferences of different audiences. Often, what looks most appealing, isn't the most effective when it comes to analysis. Therefore, work and attention to detail in this phase can allow for a single data set to be able to meet both priorities. Create effective and appealing visualizations in addition to providing the structure needed for deeper analysis.

The sample Marketing Data Set contains two simple data tables. The first one is the trending of a main metric or Key Performance Indicator (KPI) against a target or goal. This is a very common use case. Sometimes a table format is desired as multiple metrics and factors can be viewed and applying conditional formatting and visual indicators can make an effective visual to understand the status of a metric. A graphical format set up in a time series either with a bar or line chart can be helpful in visualize how a metric is trending over time. In this case a combination bar and line graph was used with the goal being set as a line and the actual metric as a bar. The color of the series output can also be changed through the basic color formatting functionality.

Removing the sheet gridlines inside of the View menu is a method to clear the gridlines when displaying the resulting summary views.

Different color scales and chart types were also implemented in this section. Microsoft Excel makes it easy to change between different chart types, formats, and themes. Can easily change from a bar to a line chart. A pie chart or a sorted bar chart works well for data that has categories and it is desire to see the relative values of each category compared to the others.

# Module 7

- Text to Columns
- Drop Down using Data Validation
- Special Formatting Example – Phone Numbers

# Data Entry and Organization

This Module begins the journey of effective data entry and some useful formulas. Formatting the phone number will enable easy to view fields, while facilitating the data entry process. The helpful text to column features will be utilized to separate out address components to different columns. The Join operation will be used to combine the last name and first name together.

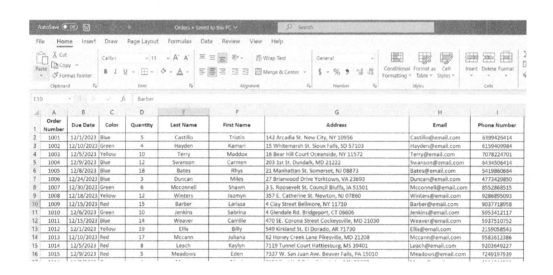

| Order Number | Due Date | Color | Quantity | Last Name | First Name | Address | Email | Phone Number |
|---|---|---|---|---|---|---|---|---|
| 1001 | 12/1/2023 | Blue | 5 | Castillo | Tristin | 142 Arcadia St. New City, NY 10956 | Castillo@email.com | 6399426414 |
| 1002 | 12/10/2023 | Green | 4 | Hayden | Kamari | 15 Whitemarsh St. Sioux Falls, SD 57103 | Hayden@email.com | 6159409984 |
| 1003 | 12/5/2023 | Yellow | 10 | Terry | Maddox | 16 Bear Hill Court Oceanside, NY 11572 | Terry@email.com | 7078224701 |
| 1004 | 12/9/2023 | Blue | 12 | Swanson | Carmen | 203 1st St. Dundalk, MD 21222 | Swanson@email.com | 6434506414 |
| 1005 | 12/8/2023 | Blue | 18 | Bates | Rhys | 21 Manhattan St. Somerset, NJ 08873 | Bates@email.com | 5419860664 |
| 1006 | 12/24/2023 | Blue | 3 | Duncan | Miles | 27 Briarwood Drive Yorktown, VA 23693 | Duncan@email.com | 4773429850 |
| 1007 | 12/30/2023 | Green | 6 | Mcconnell | Shawn | 3 S. Roosevelt St. Council Bluffs, IA 51501 | Mcconnell@email.com | 8552868515 |
| 1008 | 12/18/2023 | Yellow | 12 | Winters | Jazmyn | 357 E. Catherine St. Newton, NJ 07860 | Winters@email.com | 9286895093 |
| 1009 | 12/15/2023 | Red | 15 | Barber | Larissa | 4 Clay Street Bellmore, NY 11710 | Barber@email.com | 9037718958 |
| 1010 | 12/6/2023 | Green | 10 | Jenkins | Sabrina | 4 Glendale Rd. Bridgeport, CT 06606 | Jenkins@email.com | 5953412117 |
| 1011 | 12/15/2023 | Blue | 14 | Weaver | Camille | 470 SE. Corona Street Cockeysville, MD 21030 | Weaver@email.com | 5937510752 |
| 1012 | 12/1/2023 | Yellow | 19 | Ellis | Billy | 549 Kirkland St. El Dorado, AR 71730 | Ellis@email.com | 2159058543 |
| 1013 | 12/10/2023 | Red | 17 | Mccann | Juliana | 62 Honey Creek Lane Pikesville, MD 21208 | Mccann@email.com | 9583612386 |
| 1014 | 12/5/2023 | Red | 8 | Leach | Kaylyn | 7119 Tunnel Court Hattiesburg, MS 39401 | Leach@email.com | 9203649227 |
| 1015 | 12/9/2023 | Red | 5 | Meadows | Eden | 7337 W. San Juan Ave. Beaver Falls, PA 15010 | Meadows@email.com | 7249197939 |

| Select All Phone Numbers, Click Format, More Number Formats, Speical & Choose Phone Number |
| --- |
| **Phone Number** |
| (639) 942-6414 |
| (615) 940-9984 |
| (707) 822-4701 |
| 6434506414 |
| 5419860664 |
| 4773429850 |
| 8552868515 |
| 9286895093 |
| 9037718958 |
| 5953412117 |

# Text to Columns 2 Times

| Address |
| --- |
| 142 Arcadia St. New City, NY 10956 |
| 15 Whitemarsh St. Sioux Falls, SD 57103 |
| 16 Bear Hill Court. Oceanside, NY 11572 |
| 203 1st St. Dundalk, MD 21222 |
| 21 Manhattan St. Somerset, NJ 08873 |
| 27 Briarwood Drive. Yorktown, VA 23693 |
| 3 S Roosevelt St. Council Bluffs, IA 51501 |
| 357 E Catherine St. Newton, NJ 07860 |
| 4 Clay Street. Bellmore, NY 11710 |
| 4 Glendale Rd. Bridgeport, CT 06606 |
| 470 SE Corona Street. Cockeysville, MD 21030 |
| 549 Kirkland St. El Dorado, AR 71730 |
| 62 Honey Creek Lane. Pikesville, MD 21208 |
| 7119 Tunnel Court. Hattiesburg, MS 39401 |
| 7337 W San Juan Ave. Beaver Falls, PA 15010 |
| 7484 East Hall Drive. Prior Lake, MN 55372 |
| 758 Brickyard Court. Berwyn, IL 60402 |
| 763 Franklin Lane. Elk Grove Village, IL 60007 |
| 7703 Summit Ave. Schenectady, NY 12302 |
| 8033 Sunbeam Drive. Summerville, SC 29483 |
| 1 High Noon St. Adrian, MI 49221 |
| 114 North Bedford Street. Chicago Heights, IL 60411 |

**Convert Text to Columns Wizard - Step 2 of 3**

This screen lets you set the delimiters your data contains. You can see how your text is affected in the preview below.

Delimiters
- ☐ Tab
- ☐ Semicolon          ☐ Treat consecutive delimiters as one
- ☑ Comma              Text qualifier: "
- ☐ Space
- ☑ Other: .

Data preview

| 142 Arcadia St | New City | NY 10956 |
| 15 Whitemarsh St | Sioux Falls | SD 57103 |
| 16 Bear Hill Court | Oceanside | NY 11572 |
| 203 1st St | Dundalk | MD 21222 |
| 21 Manhattan St | Somerset | NJ 08873 |
| 27 Briarwood Drive | Yorktown | VA 23693 |

Cancel      < Back      Next >      Finish

---

| | |
| --- | --- |
| NY 10956 | |
| SD 57103 | |
| NY 11572 | |
| MD 21222 | |
| NJ 08873 | |
| VA 23693 | |
| IA 51501 | |
| NJ 07860 | |
| NY 11710 | |
| CT 06606 | |
| MD 21030 | |
| AR 71730 | |
| MD 21208 | |
| MS 39401 | |
| PA 15010 | |
| MN 55372 | |
| IL 60402 | |
| IL 60007 | |
| NY 12302 | |
| SC 29483 | |
| MI 49221 | |
| IL 60411 | |

**Convert Text to Columns Wizard - Step 2 of 3**

This screen lets you set the delimiters your data contains. You can see how your

Delimiters
- ☐ Tab
- ☐ Semicolon          ☑ Treat consecutive delimiters as one
- ☐ Comma              Text qualifier: "
- ☑ Space
- ☐ Other: .

Data preview

| | NY | 10956 |
| --- | --- | --- |
| | SD | 57103 |
| | NY | 11572 |
| | MD | 21222 |

Cancel      < Back

# Create a Drop-Down Box using Data Validation

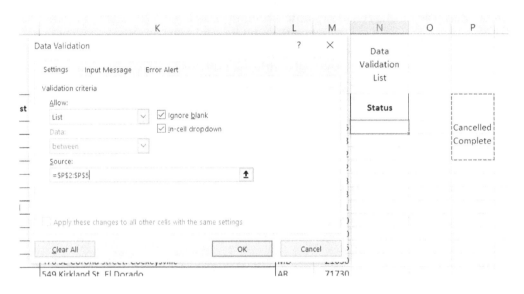

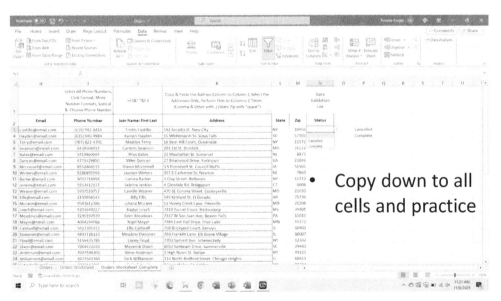

- ## Copy down to all cells and practice

# Summary: Module 7

Another feature within the formatting menu is "special" formats. The example in this module looked at formatting the phone numbers into a phone format. This helps from the data entry perspective as the numbers can be entered without putting in the special characters like parenthesis and hyphen, This can save time on the data entry piece and also help reduce errors of extra spaces etc. Another example of a special format that is available is a zip code. There are custom formats that can be created to match a particular format within a data set.

Text to Columns can be utilized to separate a column of data out into separate columns. In this case the address was separate into the address, city, state and zip code. This example used the delimiters, and a two-step process was able to complete the splitting process. It is also possible to used a fixed width and pull the lines to desired spots. The window allows a preview of the result prior to completing the operation. Since this operation located within the data tab creates extra columns it is helpful if there are spaces available to the right of the column being separated. This example, copy and pasted the column to the end column of the data set.

The Data Validation command was used to create a drop-down box. In this example, the status of the order can be updated with options that were typed in separate cells and then referenced within the drop-down box source data. Drop Down boxes can be helpful with data entry to minimize typing and while helping improve consistency of spelling.

# Module 8

- Pivot Table Introduction

# Pivot Table Introduction

An introduction to fundamental Pivot Tables and Chart creation

## Go To:
## Insert > Pivot Table > Select Table Range

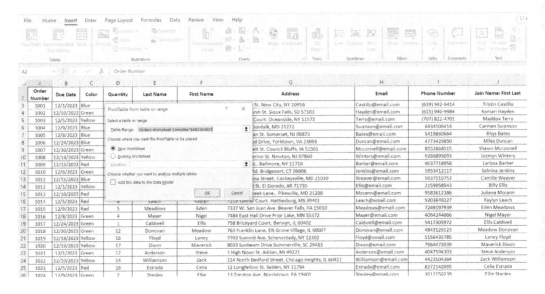

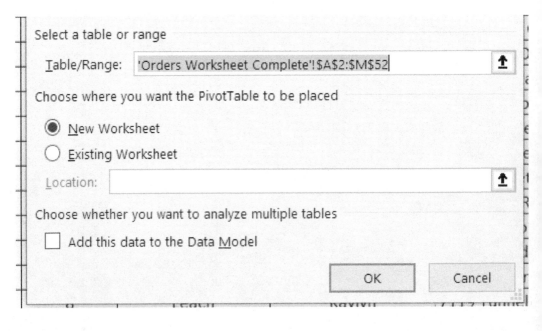

# Pivot Table basic layout

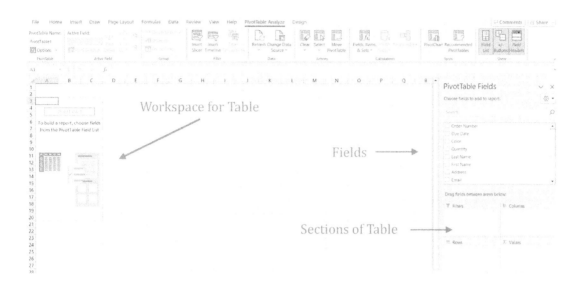

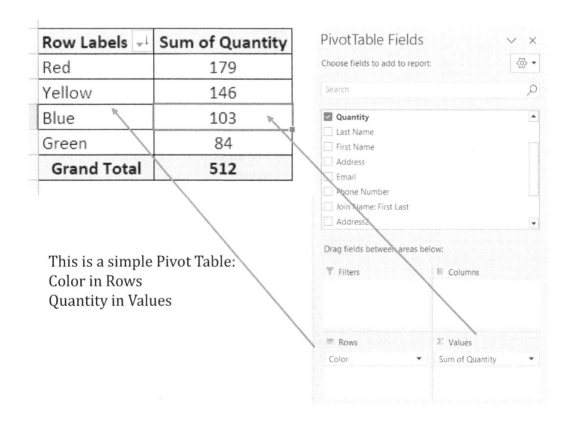

This is a simple Pivot Table:
Color in Rows
Quantity in Values

# Pivot Tables: Working with the different fields

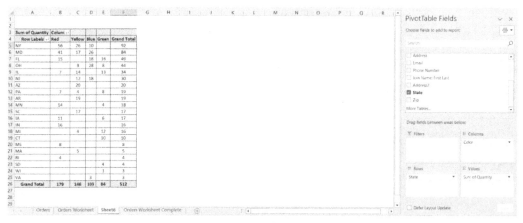

Re-arranged the Pivot Table
- Color in Column
- State in Row
- Quantity in Values
- Sorted by Quantity

Added First Last Name in
Report Filter

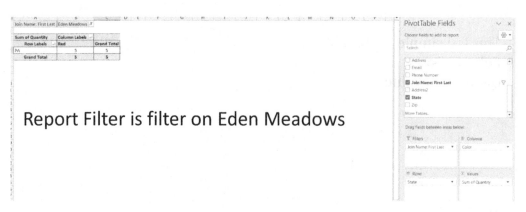

Report Filter is filter on Eden Meadows

# Pivot Tables: Calculations

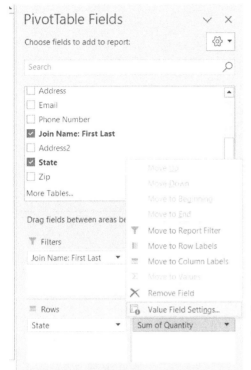

- Value Field Settings
- In the Value Field
- Can change to different operations

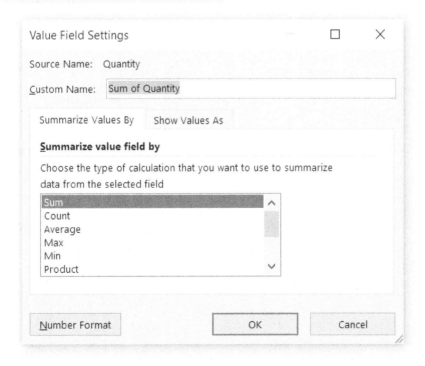

# Pivot Tables: Re-arrange and Sort

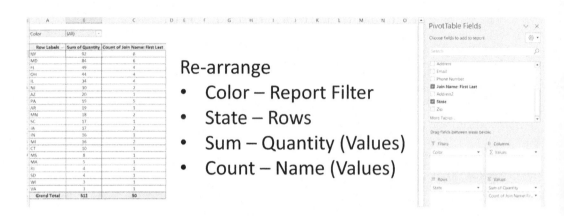

Re-arrange
- Color – Report Filter
- State – Rows
- Sum – Quantity (Values)
- Count – Name (Values)

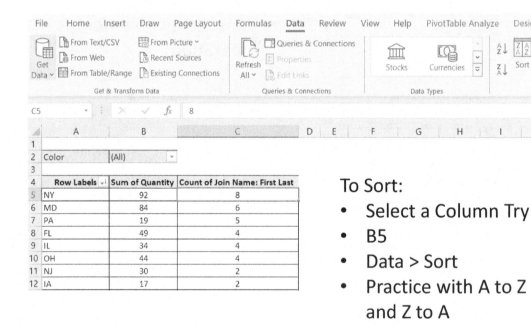

To Sort:
- Select a Column Try
- B5
- Data > Sort
- Practice with A to Z and Z to A
- Repeat for C5

# Pivot Tables: Re-arrange and Set up for a Chart

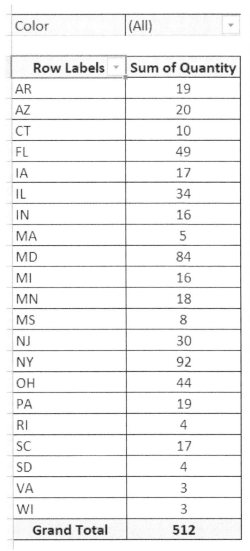

| Color | (All) |
|---|---|

| Row Labels | Sum of Quantity |
|---|---|
| AR | 19 |
| AZ | 20 |
| CT | 10 |
| FL | 49 |
| IA | 17 |
| IL | 34 |
| IN | 16 |
| MA | 5 |
| MD | 84 |
| MI | 16 |
| MN | 18 |
| MS | 8 |
| NJ | 30 |
| NY | 92 |
| OH | 44 |
| PA | 19 |
| RI | 4 |
| SC | 17 |
| SD | 4 |
| VA | 3 |
| WI | 3 |
| Grand Total | 512 |

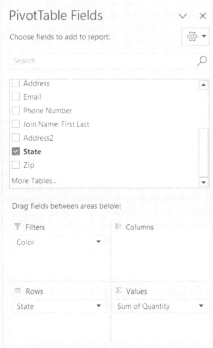

Rearrange Pivot Table
- Color – Report Filter
- Rows – State
- Values - Quantity

## Pivot Tables: Insert a Chart

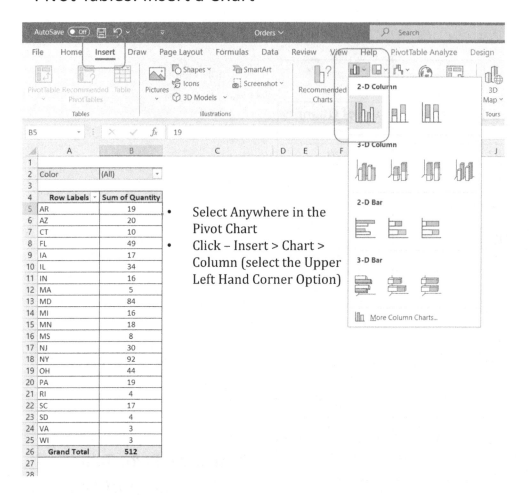

- Select Anywhere in the Pivot Chart
- Click – Insert > Chart > Column (select the Upper Left Hand Corner Option)

# Pivot Tables: Chart and Use Report Filter to Filter the Chart

| Color | (All) |
|---|---|

| Row Labels | Sum of Quantity |
|---|---|
| AR | 19 |
| AZ | 20 |
| CT | 10 |
| FL | 49 |
| IA | 17 |
| IL | 34 |
| IN | 16 |
| MA | 5 |
| MD | 84 |
| MI | 16 |
| MN | 18 |
| MS | 8 |
| NJ | 30 |
| NY | 92 |
| OH | 44 |
| PA | 19 |
| RI | 4 |
| SC | 17 |
| SD | 4 |
| VA | 3 |
| WI | 3 |
| **Grand Total** | **512** |

# Filtered by Blue – Report Filter

| Color | Blue |
|---|---|

| Row Labels | Sum of Quantity |
|---|---|
| FL | 18 |
| MD | 26 |
| NJ | 18 |
| NY | 10 |
| OH | 28 |
| VA | 3 |
| **Grand Total** | **103** |

# Summary: Module 8

A Pivot Table is a powerful tool within Microsoft Excel that can be used to summarize data with considerable flexibility. The tables are interactive, and the data can be re-arranged very easily into different table layouts. Several functions are available that include counting, summing and sorting. Another advantage of pivot tables is the ability to summarize large amounts of data efficiently. Charts can be created very easily from pivot tables, and they also have interactive ability.

There is a section in the pivot table view that is a workspace where the resulting table will appear. The field list shows all of the columns within the selected range and there is a section place to place row and column data as well as on overall report filter and then a values section to specify the field and desired operation.

When setting up pivot tables the table has to be continuous with every field having a column header, if there is a space in the table headers and error message will appear.

With the interactive nature of pivot tables, it is recommended to just dive in and start working with them. Sometimes new users hesitate and worry about being wrong. It is so easy to re-arrange, that it is recommended to try putting various fields in different areas and compare the different outputs obtained.

# Module 9

- Working with Data Sets: Social Media
  - Filters: Adding and Clearing
  - SUMIFS
  - Pivot Tables with Dates
  - Formatting Pivot Tables and Charts
  - Filters and Slicers
  - IFERROR

# Working with Data Sets – Social Media

This next data set will be utilizing social media data.  This exercise will utilize search features, pivot tables and filters.

| Date Recorded | Location | Reach | Followers | Total Follwers | Account Type | Last |
|---|---|---|---|---|---|---|
| 5/13/2022 | West | 50 | 20 | | | |
| 5/13/2022 | East | 12 | | | | |
| 5/13/2022 | North | 51 | | | | |
| 5/13/2022 | East | | | | | |
| 5/23/2022 | West | 20 | 11 | | | |
| 5/23/2022 | East | 8 | | | | |
| 5/23/2022 | North | 22 | | | | |
| 5/23/2022 | East | | | | | |
| 5/29/2022 | West | 20 | 12 | | | |
| 5/29/2022 | East | 3 | | | | |
| 5/29/2022 | North | 16 | | | | |
| 5/29/2022 | East | | | | | |
| 5/29/2022 | South | 62 | | | | |
| 6/4/2022 | West | 15 | 15 | 166 | | |
| 6/4/2022 | East | 14 | | 20 | | |
| 6/4/2022 | North | 34 | | 126 | | |

The Account Type Field needs to be populated and a filter will be used to accomplish this task. The East and West are New accounts, and the North and South are Transferred.  They will be named accordingly.

To set up the Filter.  Put the curser in the row where the filter will be placed and click Data Filter.

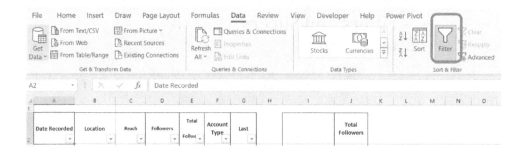

Select the arrow on the Location column and select the East and West check boxes, click Ok. In the account type field type in New and copy and paste it down while the filter is still on. Repeat this step for North and South populating those fields with Transfer.

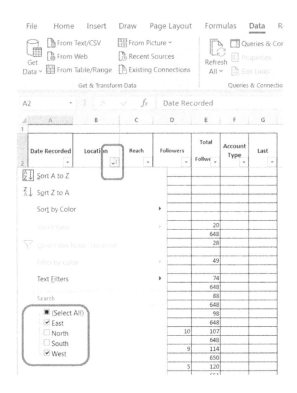

| Date Recorded | Location | Reach | Followers | Total Follwers | Account Type | Last |
|---|---|---|---|---|---|---|
| 1/3/2023 | West | 36 | 1 | | New | |
| 1/3/2023 | West | 32 | 1 | 304 | New | |
| 1/9/2023 | West | 17 | 4 | 307 | New | |
| 1/16/2023 | West | 298 | 1 | 306 | New | |
| 1/23/2023 | West | 82 | 2 | 310 | New | |
| 1/30/2023 | West | 384 | 4 | 310 | New | |
| 2/6/2023 | West | 22 | 2 | 312 | New | |
| 2/14/2023 | West | 18 | 5 | 315 | New | |
| 3/20/2023 | West | 19 | | 317 | New | |
| 3/18/2023 | West | 25 | 4 | 320 | New | |
| 4/16/2023 | West | 20 | 6 | 329 | New | |
| 4/23/2023 | West | 13 | 2 | 330 | New | |
| 4/29/2023 | West | 97 | 2 | 332 | New | |
| 5/9/2023 | West | 43 | 0 | 332 | New | Last |

The Clear option will remove the filtered selected while still keeping the filter option in place. Clicking filter (the larger funnel) will remove the filter completely from the columns.

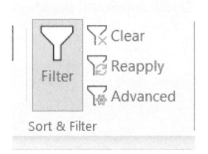

When the data is pulled from the social media accounts and entered. A date range is used to get the Reach and Followers for that time frame. However, the total followers is a single number that is captured. So a formula will be used to pull the last value with the assumption that when the data is entered the person moves the last indicator to the most recent set of entries.

| Date Recorded | Location | Reach | Followers | Total Follwe | Account Type | Last |
|---|---|---|---|---|---|---|
| 4/23/2023 | South | 102 | 3 | 502 | Transfer | |
| 4/23/2023 | West | 13 | 2 | 330 | New | |
| 4/29/2023 | East | 31 | 0 | 161 | New | |
| 4/29/2023 | East | 14 | 2 | 713 | New | |
| 4/29/2023 | North | 26 | 2 | 304 | Transfer | |
| 4/29/2023 | South | 319 | 2 | 501 | Transfer | |
| 4/29/2023 | West | 97 | 2 | 332 | New | |
| 5/9/2023 | East | 16 | 0 | 161 | New | Last |
| 5/9/2023 | East | 12 | 1 | 713 | New | Last |
| 5/9/2023 | North | 45 | 0 | 305 | Transfer | Last |
| 5/9/2023 | South | 585 | 0 | 501 | Transfer | Last |
| 5/9/2023 | West | 43 | 0 | 332 | New | Last |

SUMIFS – this is a power formula that will total up a specific value based on criteria. Multiple criteria can be specified. In this case, the total followers will be calculated by Location ensuring that only the last entry is pulled.

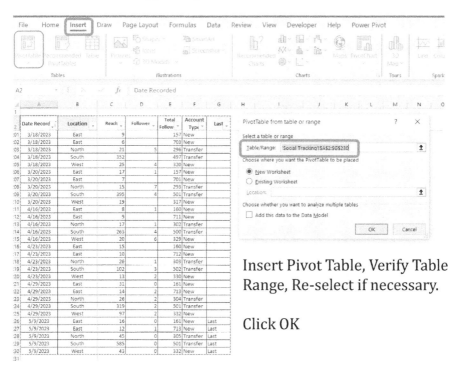

| | J3 | | | | $f_x$ | =SUMIFS(E:E,B:B,I3,G4:G:G,"Last") | | | | |
|---|---|---|---|---|---|---|---|---|---|---|

| | A | B | C | D | E | F | G | H | I | J |
|---|---|---|---|---|---|---|---|---|---|---|
| 2 | Date Record | Location | Reach | Follower | Total Follow | Account Type | Last | | | Total Followers |
| 3 | 5/13/2022 | East | 12 | | | New | | | North | 305 |
| 4 | 5/13/2022 | East | | | | New | | | South | 501 |
| 5 | 5/13/2022 | North | 51 | | | Transfer | | | East | 874 |
| 6 | 5/13/2022 | West | 50 | 20 | | New | | | West | 332 |
| 7 | 5/23/2022 | East | 8 | | | New | | | | |

SUMIFS – review of the highlighted formula shows that the formulas adds up Column E (Total Followers) when the criteria location matches that in column I and in column G, the last note is indicated.

The formula is then copied to remaining cells. Just make sure to check it is doing what you intend. Filters are a good way to verify results. In this case, the entire columns were chosen so Freezing or absolute reference was inherent.

The data is now set up, let's proceed to creation of Pivot Tables.

Insert Pivot Table, Verify Table Range, Re-select if necessary.

Click OK

Set up the Pivot Table as shown below.  Location in report filter, Sum of Reach in Values and Date Recorded in Rows.

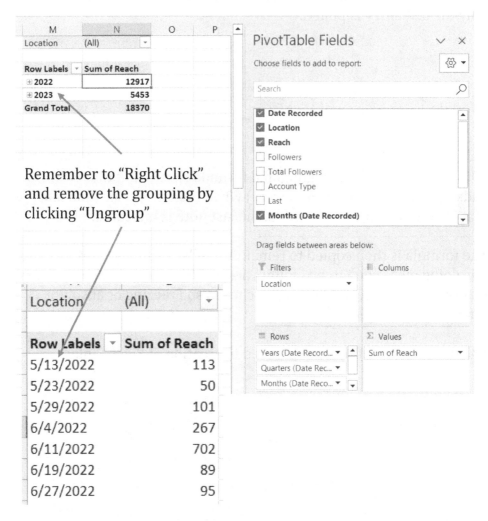

Remember to "Right Click" and remove the grouping by clicking "Ungroup"

Create a Line Chart from the Pivot Table.  After placing the cursor anywhere in the Pivot Table, click Insert > Line Chart.

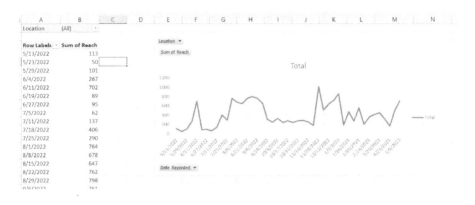

The following sequence is a series of steps formatting the graph.

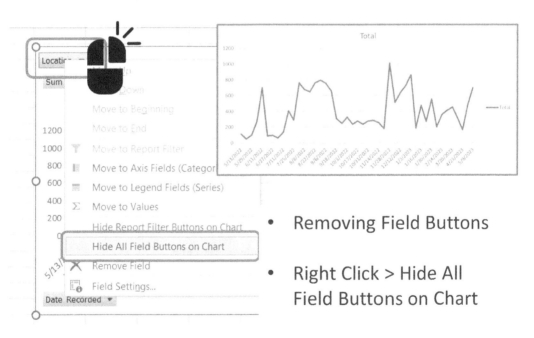

- **Removing Field Buttons**

- **Right Click > Hide All Field Buttons on Chart**

The field buttons can be helpful; however, they do take up space. This is an optional preference.

The chart title was changed and made Bold Black Font and the Gridlines were removed. Also, the Legend saying "Total" was removed.

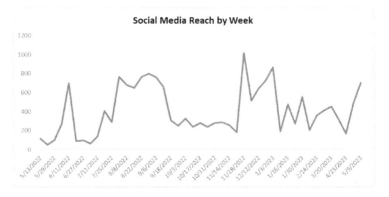

A text box is going to be added to the chart that will update when the filter for location is changed. It is key to select the graph first prior to adding the text box so that it is integrated into the chart. Once the chart is selected, to confirm that the chart has been selected prior to adding the text box, look for the little circles as indicated by the circle surrounding them.

After the chart is selected, click Insert > Text Box

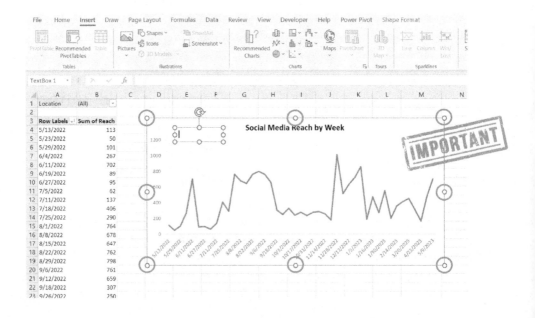

This step isn't hard but is tricky...Once it is inside the text box, get the cursor to flash, then go to the formula bar and put = and select the cell B1 as this is the cell reference that will go in the text box.

The purpose of this is to have a text box on the graph that will change and update when the filter changes.

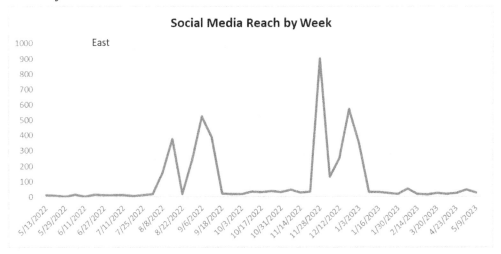

The graph below shows that the data and graph is filtered on East. The text box has been sized, centered and formatted with yellow fill.

## Social Media Reach by Week

East

The pivot table can be copied and pasted to another cell and then just change the fields. In this case, everything was kept the same except for the values. They were changed form Reach to Followers.

A new graph was created for this pivot with the same steps of selecting a cell within the pivot table and clicking Insert Chart. In this case a bar chart was selected.

The Pivot Chart below was formatted with a bar chart, changing the format fill of the bars, clearing gridlines, legend, and buttons. In this example, 2 text boxes were added. One for the filter of location and also one for the total followers.

To get the total followers, the sumifs formula was used to get the total followers by location. Looking closer at the formula the iferror statement was used to put a blank if the formula doesn't return ad result which would be the case when All is selected

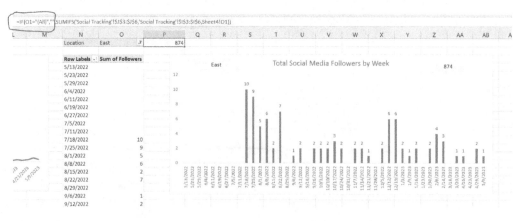

The next example of functionality that will be added is called a slicer. It is a filtering concept that works with pivot tables and tables that are dynamic.

## Insert > Slicer

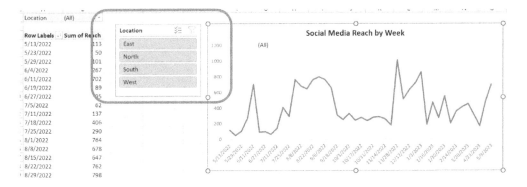

One great aspect of slicers is that they can be attached to multiple pivot tables. This is great when there a multiple tables and charts that are related.

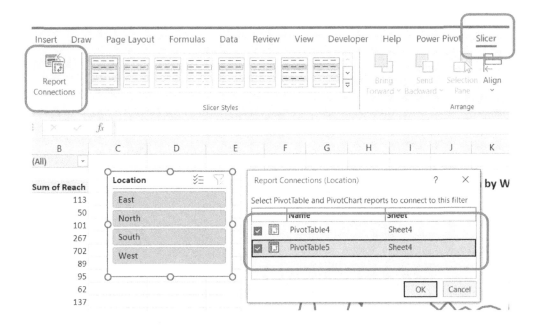

A Timeline can also be added which is another type of slicer. Insert > Timeline. See below, it can be used to filter pivot tables and charts on different time frames with a slider style timeline.

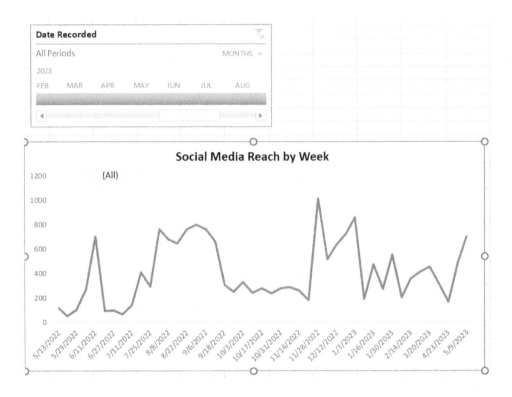

# Summary: Module 9

Module 9 utilizes a data set that includes social media followers and reach as the main metric being analyzed. This data set simulates a practical real-life data set as some categorization is needed prior to working with the data. There are four locations included and two of them represent new accounts and two are transferred accounts. In order to add this, a filter was utilized.

Once the filter is in pace and the location drop-down is view, the select all box can be unselected and then then the two locations that have the same account type can be selected together. The column with the account type can easily be updated by copying down the type. This step is repeated for the other two locations.

One great aspect of use case sample data, like this set of social media data, is that it demonstrates how many different principles and commands can be utilized to accomplish and end result and tell a story with the data.

There are two different ways to remove a filter. One is to completely remove it from the fields which can be completed by clicking again on Data > Filter. This is the same way it was put on; it can be un-selected to remove. Clearing the filter is different. The clear filter icon will clear any set filters that are on one or more columns while keeping the filter functionality on the table intact. This option is good if additional filtering will take place. While it is no problem to add and remove filters completely, it just represents and small extra step.

The SUMIFS formula is a very helpful operation that can total a column of data based on multiple criteria. The convention of the formula is to first enter the range that will be totaled then enter the range of the first criteria and the matching value in the table. The range in each part of the formula must match for example, if the sum range goes from A2:D5000 all of the ranges for the subsequent criteria must be the same.A2:D5000. This is one of those subtle nuances that can cause a formula not to work if the ranges don't match.

A pivot table was also set up in this section to look at the trends of the social media followers and reach over time. Upon using dates in the row settings, Excel grouped them into years. This highlights the grouping functionality. To remove the grouping, it is a simple "right-click" on the date (year) and click ungroup. If grouping is desired, there are options for Years, Months, Weeks, Quarters etc. This demonstrates the flexibility with Excel functionality.

The pivot charts have a default setting with field buttons that allow for live filter directly on the chart that will also update the corresponding table. In some cases, users prefer to clear this space. To do so, right click on the field button and click, hide all field buttons.

# Summary: Module 9 (continued)

Adding dynamic text boxes to Pivot Tables is a great way to customize the graph while making it easier to conduct dynamic analysis without losing track of the filters. This example showed brining in the location filter as well as the total followers that resulted from the sumifs formula.

There are several small details that are required to make the text boxes become an integral part of the pivot table. One is ensuring that the chart is selected prior to adding the text box. Then with the cursor live within the text box, click inside the formula bar and enter an = signs then select the cell that the desired heading is coming from. While not difficult, there are some subtleties that make this concept work.

Slicers and Timelines are another form of filters that can be used to filter data. The advantage of these over regular report filters is that they can be applied to multiple pivot tables and charts that have a common criteria field. This is great for setting up dashboards or graphical summaries. To connect many pivot tables and charts to the slicer or timeline, go to slicer, report connections and select the pivot tables desired. To obtain the pivot table number, click on the Pivot Table and go to Pivot Table Analyze then look in the far-right box as it will show the pivot table number.

# Module 10

- Working with Data Sets: Phone Call Data
  - Freeze Panes and Scrolling
  - Cleaning Data: Text to Value
  - Go To, Find, Find and Replace
  - Paste Menu Overview
  - Count, Sum and Subtotal
  - Status Bar Usage
  - Decimals and Rounding

# Working with Data Sets

Cell phone data example will utilize find replace, filter, subtotal formulas along with additional Pivot Table use cases. Data reformatting techniques will be used as this data is system generated and some of the formats need to be adjusted. This is a reality of many data sets that are exported or downloaded from systems.

It is always a good idea to review the data set especially when it comes out of a system. The first step in order to allow scrolling while continuing to see the headers is Freeze Panes.

There are 3 types of freezing panes and the visual that the Excel menu provides is very helpful. The cursor was place in B2 and the 1st option was selected.

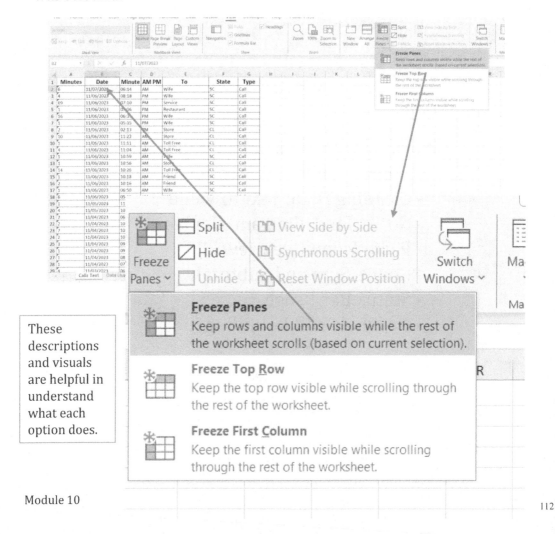

These descriptions and visuals are helpful in understand what each option does.

Freezing Panes (continued)

While freezing panes is quite helpful when working with a
spreadsheet, it is quite common to accidentally freeze the panes in a
random location and it will appear that you can't access or scroll to
certain parts of the spreadsheet.

A quick check inside View "Freeze" can allow for a quick check. If it
says "Unfreeze" that is the indicator that freeze panes is on. You can
just click once to remove it, double check the cursor location and click
again to put it on.

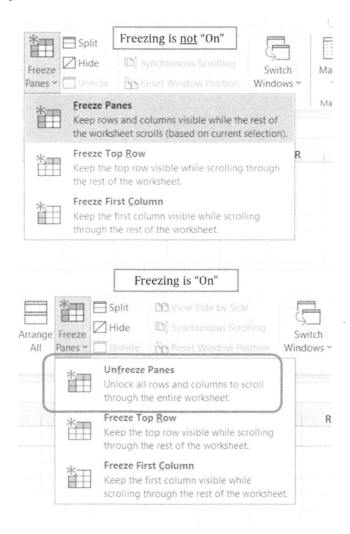

Reviewing the dataset

A quick scroll and glance at the data can often reveal some opportunities for cleaning it up. It isn't always possible to catch everything, however, it is a good practice to continue to hone this skill.

A few things are noticed, there is a little green arrow in the minute column which is an indicator that it is a text value and Excel recognizes that it has numbers, they just aren't values. There is a state CL which is not a state but indicator of Toll Free. Some of the Minutes are blank, as well as some of the states. We will work through each one of these.

| Minute | Date | Minut | AM Pl | To | State | Type |
|---|---|---|---|---|---|---|
| 1 | 10/27/2023 | 10:40 | AM | Friend | VA | Call |
| 3 | 10/27/2023 | 10:29 | AM | Wife | SC | Call |
| 3 | 10/27/2023 | 09:23 | AM | Wife | SC | Call |
| 1 | 10/27/2023 | 09:13 | AM | Service | SC | Call |
| 1 | 10/27/2023 | 08:43 | AM | Restaurant | SC | Call |
| 3 | 10/27/2023 | 08:11 | AM | Friend | SC | Call |
| 1 | 10/27/2023 | 08:11 | AM | Friend | VA | Call |
| 3 | 10/27/2023 | 08:07 | AM | Restaurant | CL | Call |
| 4 | 10/27/2023 | 07:37 | AM | Wife | SC | Call |
| 1 | 10/27/2023 | 07:14 | AM | Restaurant | SC | Call |
| 1 | 10/27/2023 | 06:45 | AM | Restaurant | SC | Call |
| 1 | 10/27/2023 | 05:55 | AM | Wife | SC | Call |
| 3 | 10/27/2023 | 05:41 | AM | Wife | SC | Call |
| 5 | 10/27/2023 | 05:18 | AM | Wife | SC | Call |
| 2 | 10/27/2023 | 05:10 | AM | Wife | SC | Call |
| | 11/06/2023 | 07:18 | PM | Mother | VA | Text |
| | 11/06/2023 | 07:16 | PM | Mother | SC | Text |
| | 11/06/2023 | 07:01 | PM | Father | SC | Text |
| | 11/06/2023 | 06:59 | PM | Mother | VA | Text |
| | 11/06/2023 | 02:19 | PM | Wife | SC | Text |
| | 11/06/2023 | 02:10 | PM | Mother | SC | Text |

| Minutes | Date | Minut | AM Pl | To | State | Type |
|---|---|---|---|---|---|---|
| | 10/31/2023 | 03:10 | PM | Mother | | Text |
| | 10/31/2023 | 01:01 | PM | Mother | | Text |
| | 10/31/2023 | 10:16 | AM | Mother | | Text |
| | 10/31/2023 | 09:29 | AM | Mother | | Text |
| | 10/31/2023 | 08:07 | AM | Mother | | Text |
| | 10/31/2023 | 07:31 | AM | Brother | | Text |
| | 10/30/2023 | 07:28 | PM | Mother | | Text |
| | 10/30/2023 | 06:49 | PM | Friend | FL | Text |
| | 10/30/2023 | 04:29 | PM | Mother | | Text |
| | 10/30/2023 | 09:33 | AM | Mother | | Text |
| | 10/29/2023 | 04:00 | PM | Mother | | Text |
| | 10/29/2023 | 10:20 | AM | Mother | | Text |
| | 10/28/2023 | 01:51 | PM | Mother | | Text |
| | 10/27/2023 | 05:01 | PM | Mother | | Text |
| | 10/27/2023 | 11:09 | AM | Mother | | Text |
| | 10/27/2023 | 10:58 | AM | Mother | | Text |
| | 10/27/2023 | 10:15 | AM | Mother | | Text |
| | 10/27/2023 | 09:34 | AM | Mother | | Text |
| | 10/27/2023 | 09:31 | AM | Mother | | Text |
| | 10/27/2023 | 08:28 | AM | Neighbor | SC | Text |
| | 10/27/2023 | 08:27 | AM | Mother | | Text |
| | 10/27/2023 | 08:26 | AM | Mother | | Text |
| | 10/27/2023 | 08:24 | AM | Neighbor | SC | Text |

A quick scroll and glance at the data can often reveal some opportunities for cleaning it up. It isn't always possible to catch everything, however, it is a good practice to continue to hone this skill.

A few things are noticed, there is a little green arrow in the minute column which is an indicator that it is a text value and Excel recognizes that it has numbers, they just aren't values. There is a state CL which is not a state but indicator of Toll Free. Some of the Minutes are blank, as well as some of the states. We will work through each one of these.

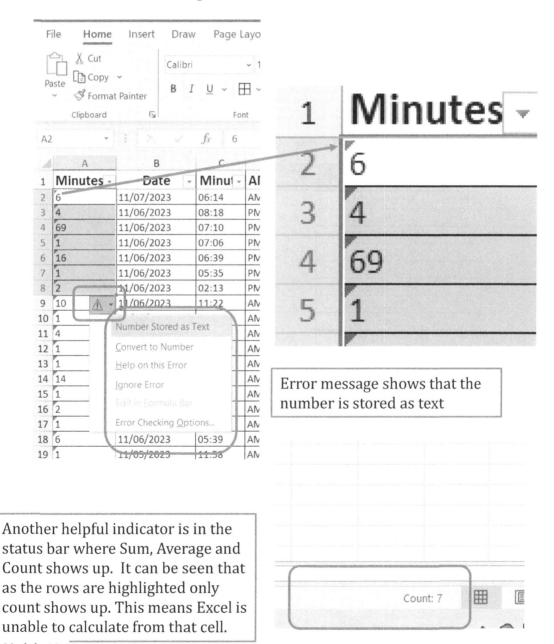

Error message shows that the number is stored as text

Another helpful indicator is in the status bar where Sum, Average and Count shows up. It can be seen that as the rows are highlighted only count shows up. This means Excel is unable to calculate from that cell.

2 Methods will be reviewed to convert the Text to Value.

One will be performed, then the undo feature will be utilized and we will perform the 2nd method.

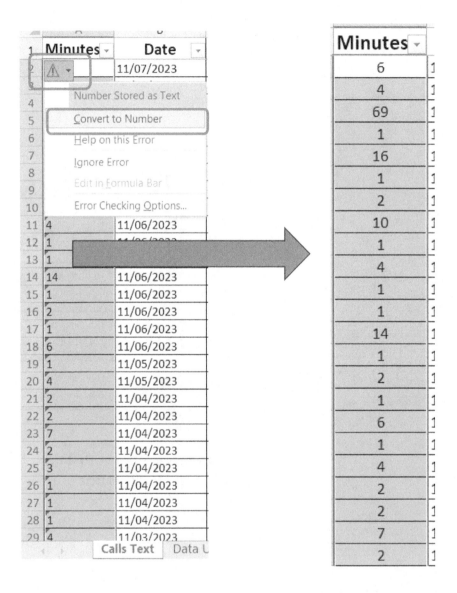

The status bar is showing calculations, after the conversion.

Average: 3.897959184    Count: 147    Sum: 573

=VALUE formula

Click the Undo icon to return the data to Text and the second method will be reviewed.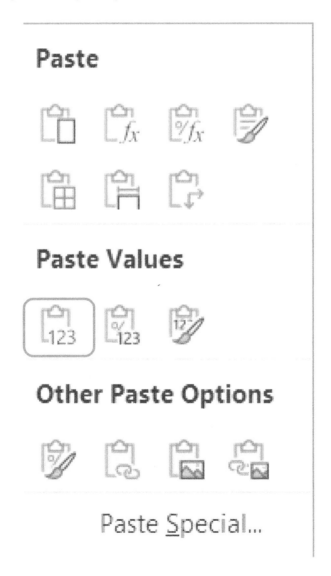

The method of using the error message for the conversion is very helpful and efficient, however, sometimes a conversion to a value is necessary and the error message is not indicated. The Value formula will be used for this.

Within the paste menu, it is good to become familiar with the different types. Often practicing with them and reviewing the results is a good exercise.

For this example, we are pasting as values which is indicated below.

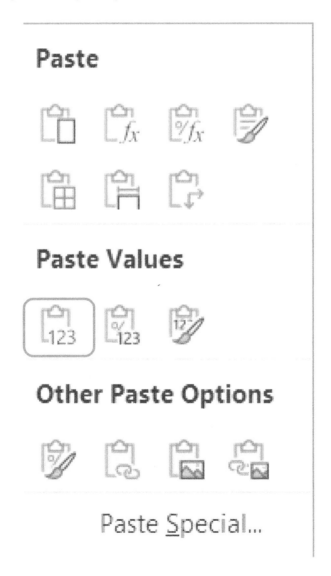

=VALUE formula

Two temporary columns were created H to perform the =Value and I to paste those values. When complete the pasted values are copied over top of those in A and rows H and I are deleted.

It may seem like extra steps and certainly compared to using the error message conversion, it is but the Value formula comes in helpful in the instances when Excel does not offer the error message and conversion.

The end result will look and operate the same wit both methods.

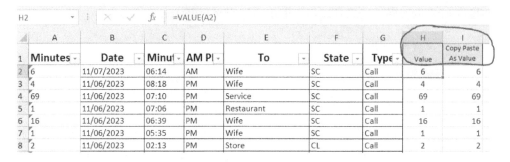

Blank Values in Minute Column

After review of the minute column it can be noticed that those that have blanks are all Text. This makes sense because the Text messages don't have a call length. This can be verified using a filter.

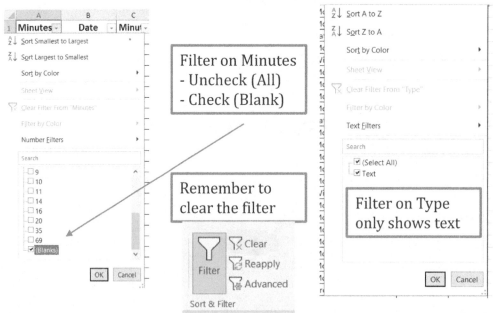

Find, Replace, Go To

The Find, Go To and Replace features have many different potential applications. There are quickly accessed using a combination of keystrokes.

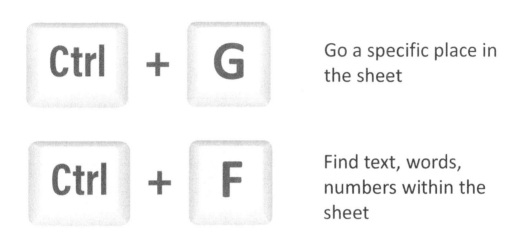

Go a specific place in the sheet

Find text, words, numbers within the sheet

For this example, the "Go To" feature will not be used, however, since it is similar to the "Find" and "Find Replace" it will be demonstrated.

Click Ctrl + G and type in the cell address and click Ok, it will take you to that spot. This is especially useful for large spreadsheets.

Replace the "CL" with Toll Free

In addition to the Find and Replace method that we are going to utilize for this exercise, a filter could also be used. State could be filtered by CL and then the words Toll Free can be typed and copied to the visible cells.

We are going to practice with using Find and Replace.

| Minutes ⌄ | Date ⌄ | Minut ⌄ | AM Pl ⌄ | To ⌄ | State ⌄ | Type ⌄ |
|---|---|---|---|---|---|---|
| 1 | 11/05/2023 | 11:58 | AM | Brother | SC | Call |
| 4 | 11/05/2023 | 10:22 | AM | Restaurant | SC | Call |
| 2 | 11/04/2023 | 06:57 | PM | Restaurant | SC | Call |
| 2 | 11/04/2023 | 10:46 | AM | Store | CL | Call |
| 7 | 11/04/2023 | 10:38 | AM | Service | CL | Call |
| 2 | 11/04/2023 | 10:30 | AM | Service | CL | Call |
| 3 | 11/04/2023 | 09:42 | AM | Restaurant | SC | Call |
| 1 | 11/04/2023 | 09:41 | AM | Store | TN | Call |
| 1 | 11/04/2023 | 08:11 | AM | Restaurant | SC | Call |
| 1 | 11/04/2023 | 07:51 | AM | Restaurant | SC | Call |
| 4 | 11/03/2023 | 06:18 | PM | Service | CL | Call |
| 5 | 11/03/2023 | 05:14 | PM | Mother | SC | Call |
| 20 | 11/03/2023 | 03:33 | PM | Store | CL | Call |
| 1 | 11/03/2023 | 08:50 | AM | Sister | SC | Call |
| 4 | 11/02/2023 | 04:50 | PM | Store | CL | Call |
| 11 | 11/02/2023 | 04:10 | PM | Restaurant | SC | Call |

Click Ctrl + F

This opens the find screen. Type in CL and click find next a few times. This has many helpful uses within Microsoft Excel. We are then going to click the Replace option and initiate replacing CL with Toll Free. It is advised to think through this prior to a mass replace as it will find anywhere the two letters CL exist and replace with Toll Free.

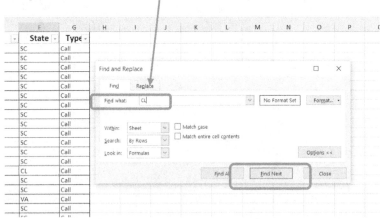

Click Ctrl + F

Select the entire column for State (in this case) that will limit the operation to the selected cells.  Once everything is entered, click Replace for  a single replace.  This is good to do a couple of times just to ensure things are working correctly.  Then can select the "Replace All".

At the end it will tell you how many replacements it made.  This is another good verification, if that number doesn't seem appropriate, further investigation may be warranted.

Click Ctrl + F

This feature has many useful purpose like looking for a specific name or record.  You can use in combination with a filter to locate specific types of records.

Within the options, you can select that it also looks inside formulas which can be helpful to look for and change references in formulas or even find mistakes.

Back to the Phone Data

| F |
|---|
| **State** |
| SC |
| SC |
| SC |
| SC |
| Toll Free |
| SC |
| VA |
| Toll Free |
| SC |
| VA |
| SC |
| SC |
| SC |
| SC |
| SC |
| VA |
| Toll Free |
| SC |

The Find and Replace has updated all the CL records in the State column with Toll Free

As a reminder, if the result doesn't look as you intended, the Undo operation will work as long as the file hasn't been saved since the replace was made. It is a good idea to check it first prior to saving. A quick scan can be helpful or even doing CTRL F a few times on Toll Free just to make sure it didn't go to any unwanted locations. ☺

| A | B | C | D | E | F |
|---|---|---|---|---|---|
| Minutes | Date | Minut | AM P| | To | State |
| | 11/03/2023 | 05:18 | PM | Mother | |
| | 11/03/2023 | 05:18 | PM | Mother | |
| | 11/03/2023 | 12:01 | PM | Mother | |
| | 11/03/2023 | 11:55 | AM | Mother | |
| | 11/02/2023 | 08:35 | PM | Mother | |
| | 11/02/2023 | 08:09 | PM | Brother | |
| | 11/02/2023 | 05:09 | PM | Mother | |
| | 11/02/2023 | 03:29 | PM | Neighbor | SC |
| | 11/02/2023 | 02:29 | PM | Mother | |
| | 11/02/2023 | 02:18 | PM | Neighbor | SC |
| | 11/02/2023 | 02:16 | PM | Mother | |
| | 11/02/2023 | 02:15 | PM | Mother | |
| | 11/02/2023 | 02:02 | PM | Neighbor | SC |
| | 11/02/2023 | 02:00 | PM | Neighbor | SC |
| | 11/01/2023 | 08:54 | PM | Mother | |
| | 11/01/2023 | 07:59 | PM | Brother | |
| | 11/01/2023 | 07:58 | PM | Mother | |
| | 11/01/2023 | 07:35 | PM | Mother | |
| | 11/01/2023 | 12:01 | PM | Mother | |
| | 10/31/2023 | 04:29 | PM | Mother | |
| | 10/31/2023 | 04:10 | PM | Mother | |
| | 10/31/2023 | 02:10 | PM | Mother | |

The last data clean up operation is the blank States

The Filter method will be used with a variation. The filter will be initiated from within the cell by "Right Click" and "Filter"

The Cell Value option was used as it will filter the value of "blank". The result is shown below. This looks the same as if we had filter at the column header level and selected blanks.

There are other helpful options, such as filtering by cell or font color.

| Minutes | Date | Minut | AM P | To | State | Type |
|---|---|---|---|---|---|---|
| | 11/03/2023 | 05:18 | PM | Mother | | Text |
| | 11/03/2023 | 05:18 | PM | Mother | | Text |
| | 11/03/2023 | 12:01 | PM | Mother | | Text |
| | 11/03/2023 | 11:55 | AM | Mother | | Text |
| | 11/02/2023 | 08:35 | PM | Mother | | Text |
| | 11/02/2023 | 08:09 | PM | Brother | | Text |
| | 11/02/2023 | 05:09 | PM | Mother | | Text |
| | 11/02/2023 | 02:29 | PM | Mother | | Text |
| | 11/02/2023 | 02:16 | PM | Mother | | Text |
| | 11/02/2023 | 02:15 | PM | Mother | | Text |
| | 11/01/2023 | 08:54 | PM | Mother | | Text |
| | 11/01/2023 | 07:59 | PM | Brother | | Text |
| | 11/01/2023 | 07:58 | PM | Mother | | Text |
| | 11/01/2023 | 07:35 | PM | Mother | | Text |
| | 11/01/2023 | 12:01 | PM | Mother | | Text |
| | 10/31/2023 | 04:29 | PM | Mother | | Text |
| | 10/31/2023 | 04:10 | PM | Mother | | Text |

Now that the table is filter by blank in State the state SC can be filled in because that is the state for the missing data points.

Type in state and copy paste to the visible cells in that column.

The Filter can be cleared, and the data set is ready to go.

| Minutes | Date | Minut | AM PI | To | State | Type |
|---|---|---|---|---|---|---|
| 6 | 11/07/2023 | 06:14 | AM | Wife | SC | Call |
| 4 | 11/06/2023 | 08:18 | PM | Wife | SC | Call |
| 69 | 11/06/2023 | 07:10 | PM | Service | SC | Call |
| 1 | 11/06/2023 | 07:06 | PM | Restaurant | SC | Call |
| 16 | 11/06/2023 | 06:39 | PM | Wife | SC | Call |
| 1 | 11/06/2023 | 05:35 | PM | Wife | SC | Call |
| 2 | 11/06/2023 | 02:13 | PM | Store | Toll Free | Call |
| 10 | 11/06/2023 | 11:22 | AM | Store | Toll Free | Call |
| 1 | 11/06/2023 | 11:11 | AM | Toll Free | Toll Free | Call |

Note

A quick note!  As we work though the different exercise, the functions, commands and features are used for a specific purpose in that example.  However, many of these are used in different combinations in other use cases and it is helpful to keep adding techniques to your skill set.  You may not remember exactly how to do it but the awareness that it exists will help you build a solid foundation to work with an apply to different scenarios.

Practice is the key!

Count, Sum, Subtotal

To prepare the sheet, Insert 5 Rows above the Data.  Select the entire row and click Insert Rows.

The row number were selected which highlight the entire row.

This is followed by "Right Click" Insert

Since 5 rows were selected, it will insert 5 blank rows.

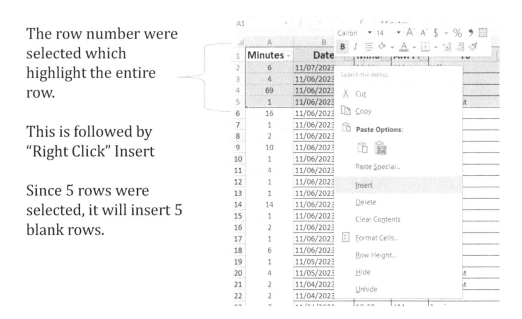

| | A | B | C | D | E | F | G |
|---|---|---|---|---|---|---|---|
| 1 | | | | | | | |
| 2 | | | | | | | |
| 3 | | | | | | | |
| 4 | | | | | | | |
| 5 | | | | | | | |
| 6 | Minutes | Date | Minut | AM Pl | To | State | Type |
| 7 | 6 | 11/07/2023 | 06:14 | AM | Wife | SC | Call |
| 8 | 4 | 11/06/2023 | 08:18 | PM | Wife | SC | Call |
| 9 | 69 | 11/06/2023 | 07:10 | PM | Service | SC | Call |
| 10 | 1 | 11/06/2023 | 07:06 | PM | Restaurant | SC | Call |
| 11 | 16 | 11/06/2023 | 06:39 | PM | Wife | SC | Call |
| 12 | 1 | 11/06/2023 | 05:35 | PM | Wife | SC | Call |

Count, Sum, Subtotal

Type the descriptions as shown below in B1 to B4 and F1 to F4 and G3.

We are going to add formulas to column A and E and compare the results in order to understand how the different functions work.

| | A | B | C | D | E | F | G |
|---|---|---|---|---|---|---|---|
| 1 | | Count | | | | Count | |
| 2 | | Subtotal Count | | | | CountA | |
| 3 | | Sum (Total) | | | | Countifs | Store |
| 4 | | Subtotal Sum (Total) | | | | Subtotal CountA | |
| 5 | | | | | | | |
| 6 | **Minutes** ⌄ | **Date** ⌄ | **Minu{** ⌄ | **AM P{** ⌄ | **To** ⌄ | **State** ⌄ | **Type** ⌄ |

The sheet below has all of the formulas with an (') in front of them. This converts them to text and shows the actual formula writing.

It can be seen highlighted in the formula a example of how the ' single quote is in front.

This technique is also helpful for moving formulas to other cells around the spreadsheet.

| A1 | | | $f_x$ | '=COUNT(A7:A215) | | | | |
|---|---|---|---|---|---|---|---|---|
| | A | B | C | D | E | F | G |
| 1 | =COUNT(A7:A215) | Count | | | =COUNT(E7:E215) | Count | |
| 2 | =SUBTOTAL(2,A7:A215) | Subtotal Count | | | =COUNTA(E7:E215) | CountA | |
| 3 | =SUM(A7:A215) | Sum (Total) | | | =COUNTIFS(E6:E215,G3) | Countifs | Store |
| 4 | =SUBTOTAL(9,A7:A215) | Subtotal Sum (Total) | | | =SUBTOTAL(3,E7:E215) | Subtotal CountA | |
| 5 | | | | | | | |
| 6 | **Minutes** ⌄ | **Date** ⌄ | **Minu{** ⌄ | **AM P{** ⌄ | **To** ⌄ | **State** ⌄ | **Type** ⌄ |

Some different filters will be added so we can observe how the different formulas behave. For reference, cells can also be highlighted and compare results in the status bar as this can be a useful quick reference.

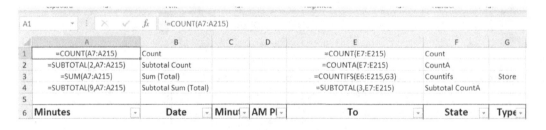

Average: 8.866666667    Count: 15    Sum: 133

With not filters on, the Count and Subtotal Count Match as do the two Sum formulas. For Columns EF only the CountA and Subtotal CountA are matching.

The Countifs is calculating only based on the criteria of Store.

We can count text and we can sum or count values. This is the same for any math function, it can only be performed on values.

This is why the first count in E1 returns 0, because it ahs to be a value and the words are not a value.

While all of the formulas go to the end of the Data, Row 215, it is return different count values. This is because we are counting the minute column which has no minutes for the text but the To column is populated for every record.

This can be validated by filter out blanks on Column A. This will be the first comparison step of this exercise.

| | A | B | C | D | E | F | G |
|---|---|---|---|---|---|---|---|
| 1 | 147 | Count | | | 0 | Count | |
| 2 | 147 | Subtotal Count | | | 209 | CountA | |
| 3 | 573 | Sum (Total) | | | 9 | Countifs | Store |
| 4 | 573 | Subtotal Sum (Total) | | | 209 | Subtotal CountA | |
| 5 | | | | | | | |
| 6 | Minutes ⌄ | Date ⌄ | Minut ⌄ | AM P⌄ | To ⌄ | State ⌄ | Type ⌄ |
| 133 | 2 | 10/27/2023 | 04:48 | PM | Wife | SC | Call |
| 134 | 7 | 10/27/2023 | 04:19 | PM | Service | Toll Free | Call |
| 135 | 8 | 10/27/2023 | 01:30 | PM | Store | SC | Call |
| 136 | 2 | 10/27/2023 | 01:27 | PM | Friend | VA | Call |
| 137 | 35 | 10/27/2023 | 10:46 | AM | Service | Toll Free | Call |
| 138 | 2 | 10/27/2023 | 10:43 | AM | Wife | SC | Call |

It can be seen that the Count and Subtotal Count for Column A and the Subtotal Count A for Column E all match at 147. The data has filtered out the blanks for ColumnA.

| | A | B | C | D | E | F | G |
|---|---|---|---|---|---|---|---|
| 1 | 147 | Count | | | 0 | Count | |
| 2 | 147 | Subtotal Count | | | 209 | CountA | |
| 3 | 573 | Sum (Total) | | | 9 | Countifs | Store |
| 4 | 573 | Subtotal Sum (Total) | | | 147 | Subtotal CountA | |
| 5 | | | | | | | |
| 6 | Minutes | Date | Minut | AM Pl | To | State | Type |
| 127 | 4 | 10/28/2023 | 07:02 | AM | Wife | SC | Call |

While the filtering makes the data not visible and only shows what is selected in the filter, the data is still there. Any formulas on that column will continue to include that data whether visible or not.

The Subtotal function allows for only the calculation of visible cell and is helpful.

This is also why the CountA is still at 209 because it is still counting the fields that are hidden as a result of the filter

Now, keep the filter on A and filter on Store in To.

It can be seen that the Subtotal Counts and the Countifs match.

| | | | | | | | |
|---|---|---|---|---|---|---|---|
| 1 | 147 | Count | | | 0 | Count | |
| 2 | 9 | Subtotal Count | | | 209 | CountA | |
| 3 | 573 | Sum (Total) | | | 9 | Countifs | Store |
| 4 | 49 | Subtotal Sum (Total) | | | 9 | Subtotal CountA | |
| 5 | | | | | | | |
| 6 | Minutes | Date | Minut | AM Pl | To | State | Type |
| 13 | 2 | 11/06/2023 | 02:13 | PM | Store | Toll Free | Call |
| 14 | 10 | 11/06/2023 | 11:22 | AM | Store | Toll Free | Call |
| 18 | 1 | 11/06/2023 | 10:56 | AM | Store | Toll Free | Call |
| 27 | 2 | 11/04/2023 | 10:46 | AM | Store | Toll Free | Call |
| 31 | 1 | 11/04/2023 | 09:41 | AM | Store | TN | Call |
| 36 | 20 | 11/03/2023 | 03:33 | PM | Store | Toll Free | Call |
| 38 | 4 | 11/02/2023 | 04:50 | PM | Store | Toll Free | Call |
| 86 | 1 | 10/30/2023 | 06:25 | PM | Store | Toll Free | Call |
| 135 | 8 | 10/27/2023 | 01:30 | PM | Store | SC | Call |
| 216 | | | | | | | |

The Subtotal Sum or Total for the minutes column is 49. This is the total minutes for the calls to the stores. This can also be seen by highlight the (9) rows in column A and looking at the status bar. The Sum of 49 and the count of 9 match the values from the relevant formulas.

In order to match the average in the status bar, we would have to put the average indicator in the subtotal formula.

| | | | | | | | | | |
|---|---|---|---|---|---|---|---|---|---|
| 1 | 147 | Count | | | 0 | Count | | | |
| 2 | 9 | Subtotal Count | | | 209 | CountA | | | |
| 3 | 573 | Sum (Total) | | | 9 | Countifs | Store | | |
| 4 | 49 | Subtotal Sum (Total) | | | 9 | Subtotal CountA | | | |
| 5 | | | | | | | | | |
| 6 | Minutes | Date | | Minut | AM PI | To | State | Type | |
| 13 | 2 | 11/06/2023 | | 02:13 | PM | Store | Toll Free | Call | |
| 14 | 10 | 11/06/2023 | | 11:22 | AM | Store | Toll Free | Call | |
| 18 | 1 | 11/06/2023 | | 10:56 | AM | Store | Toll Free | Call | |
| 27 | 2 | 11/04/2023 | | 10:46 | AM | Store | Toll Free | Call | |
| 31 | 1 | 11/04/2023 | | 09:41 | AM | Store | TN | Call | |
| 36 | 20 | 11/03/2023 | | 03:33 | PM | Store | Toll Free | Call | |
| 38 | 4 | 11/02/2023 | | 04:50 | PM | Store | Toll Free | Call | |
| 86 | 1 | 10/30/2023 | | 06:25 | PM | Store | Toll Free | Call | |
| 135 | 8 | 10/27/2023 | | 01:30 | PM | Store | SC | Call | |
| 216 | | | | | | | | | |

| | | | |
|---|---|---|---|
| 4 | | 49 | Subtotal Sum (Total) |
| 5 | | | |
| 6 | **Minutes** | **Date** | |
| 13 | 2 | 11/06/2023 | |
| 14 | 10 | 11/06/2023 | |
| 18 | 1 | 11/06/2023 | |
| 27 | 2 | 11/04/2023 | |
| 31 | 1 | 11/04/2023 | |
| 36 | 20 | 11/03/2023 | |
| 38 | 4 | 11/02/2023 | |
| 86 | 1 | 10/30/2023 | |
| 135 | 8 | 10/27/2023 | |

Highlighted the values in A

Status Bar Results

Average: 5.444444444    Count: 9    Sum: 49

The table below shows the function number for the different operations. So, if we wanted to perform, we would put a 1 in the first part of subtotal formula. This helper table shows up when typing in =Subtotal( in a valid cell within the spreadsheet.

| =subtotal( | Subtotal Count |
|---|---|

SUBTOTAL(**function_num**, ref1, ...)

| | |
|---|---|
| (....) | 1 - AVERAGE |
| (....) | 2 - COUNT |
| (....) | 3 - COUNTA |
| **Minutes** | (....) 4 - MAX |
| 5 | (....) 5 - MIN |
| 6 | (....) 6 - PRODUCT |
| 7 | (....) 7 - STDEV.S |
| 8 | (....) 8 - STDEV.P |
| 9 | (....) 9 - SUM |
| 0 | (....) 10 - VAR.S |
| | (....) 11 - VAR.P |

# Pivot Table Examples

| Row Labels | Sum of Minutes | Count of Type |
|---|---|---|
| Wife | 262 | 79 |
| Mother | 5 | 49 |
| Restaurant | 45 | 19 |
| Service | 152 | 18 |
| Friend | 24 | 12 |
| Store | 49 | 9 |
| Neighbor | | 6 |
| Brother | 3 | 6 |
| Sister | 13 | 5 |
| Father | 1 | 3 |
| Toll Free | 19 | 3 |
| **Grand Total** | **573** | **209** |

This Pivot Table Set Up Can be used to review who is getting the most calls, highest call time and most text. The slicer and / or report filter can be used to filter the table.

The Wife has the most call time and the Mother is receiving the most texts.

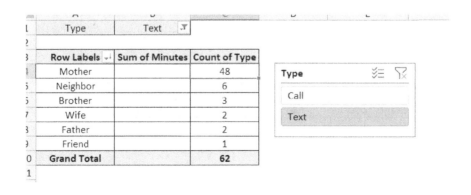

| Row Labels | Sum of Minutes | Count of Type |
|---|---|---|
| Mother | | 48 |
| Neighbor | | 6 |
| Brother | | 3 |
| Wife | | 2 |
| Father | | 2 |
| Friend | | 1 |
| **Grand Total** | | **62** |

## Calculations from Pivot Tables

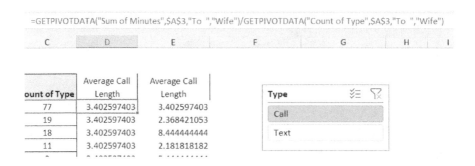

=GETPIVOTDATA("Sum of Minutes",$A$3,"To ","Wife")/GETPIVOTDATA("Count of Type",$A$3,"To ","Wife")

| | C | D | E | F | G | H | I |
|---|---|---|---|---|---|---|---|

| ount of Type | Average Call Length | Average Call Length | | Type |
|---|---|---|---|---|
| 77 | 3.402597403 | 3.402597403 | | Call |
| 19 | 3.402597403 | 2.368421053 | | |
| 18 | 3.402597403 | 8.444444444 | | Text |
| 11 | 3.402597403 | 2.181818182 | | |

The average call length can be calculated from the Pivot Table. In typing in the formula = B4 / C4 and selecting the Pivot Table cell the formula pulls in GETPIVOTDATA….. Which makes in hard to copy, read and manage. To avoid that, manually type the formula. (B4/C4)

| D4 | | | $f_x$ | =B4/C4 |
|---|---|---|---|---|

| | A | B | C | D |
|---|---|---|---|---|
| 1 | Type | Call | | |
| 2 | | | | |
| 3 | Row Labels | Sum of Minutes | Count of Type | Average Call Length |
| 4 | Wife | 262 | 77 | 3.402597403 |
| 5 | Restaurant | 45 | 19 | 2.368421053 |
| 6 | Service | 152 | 18 | 8.444444444 |
| 7 | Friend | 24 | 11 | 2.181818182 |
| 8 | Store | 49 | 9 | 5.444444444 |
| 9 | Sister | 13 | 5 | 2.6 |
| 10 | Toll Free | 19 | 3 | 6.333333333 |
| 11 | Brother | 3 | 3 | 1 |
| 12 | Father | 1 | 1 | 1 |
| 13 | Mother | 5 | 1 | 5 |
| 14 | **Grand Total** | **573** | **147** | 3.897959184 |
| 15 | | | | |

# Increasing or Decreasing Decimals vs Rounding

Copy and Paste as Values the Average Call Length into Column E. It can be seen that these values have many decimal places.

| | A | B | C | D | E |
|---|---|---|---|---|---|
| | E4 | | fx | 3.4025974025974 | |
| 1 | Type | Call | | | |
| 2 | | | | | |
| 3 | Row Labels | Sum of Minutes | Count of Type | Average Call Length | Average Call Length |
| 4 | Wife | 262 | 77 | 3.402597403 | 3.402597403 |
| 5 | Restaurant | 45 | 19 | 2.368421053 | 2.368421053 |
| 6 | Service | 152 | 18 | 8.444444444 | 8.444444444 |
| 7 | Friend | 24 | 11 | 2.181818182 | 2.181818182 |
| 8 | Store | 49 | 9 | 5.444444444 | 5.444444444 |
| 9 | Sister | 13 | 5 | 2.6 | 2.6 |
| 10 | Toll Free | 19 | 3 | 6.333333333 | 6.333333333 |
| 11 | Brother | 3 | 3 | 1 | 1 |
| 12 | Father | 1 | 1 | 1 | 1 |
| 13 | Mother | 5 | 1 | 5 | 5 |
| 14 | **Grand Total** | **573** | **147** | 3.897959184 | 3.897959184 |
| 15 | | | | | |

The visible decimal places have been decreased to 2 as seen in Column D. However, the decimals are still there. To remove, them we an apply a round function.

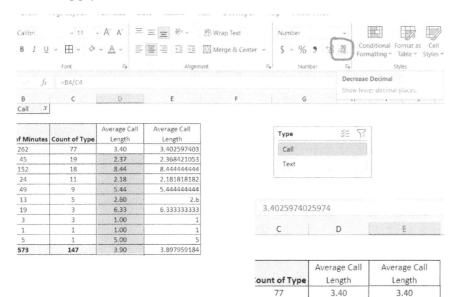

Round Up was chosen in this example and the formula convention is shown below.  =Roundup("Cell Reference", "Number of Decimal Places")

After paste as values, it can be seen that the extended decimals are no longer showing.

=ROUNDUP(E4,2)

| C | D | E | F |

| Count of Type | Average Call Length | Average Call Length | Round Up to 2 Decimal Places |
|---|---|---|---|
| 77 | 3.40 | 3.40 | 3.41 |

2.37

| C | D | E | F |

| Count of Type | Average Call Length | Average Call Length | Round Up to 2 Decimal Places |
|---|---|---|---|
| 77 | 3.40 | 3.40 | 3.41 |
| 19 | 2.37 | 2.37 | 2.37 |

# Summary: Module 10

The use case in Module 10 is a download of cell phone data. This data set required some cleansing and monitoring prior to performing analysis. There were some fields that were missing data and others had a category that needed to be changed. Filtering was an effective method to add the correct state to some of the people that received calls and were missing that field.

The short cut keys control F combined with replace can help find a specific value and change it to another value. Another helpful short cut key that was reviewed is control G that can take you directly to the address specified.

The subtotal formula is the appropriate function to use in combination with filters. This exercise demonstrated that as the subtotal will adjust to calculate only on the cells that remain after the filter. There are several mathematical operations available within the subtotal function and they are indicated by an operation number. For example, sum has the function number 9. There is a reference that pops up when initiating the formula.

This application of pivot tables along with slicers can be used for simple analysis and comparison to see who was receiving the most calls and the longest time of call.

It is also possible to create calculations outside of pivot tables while using data from within the table. To ensure that the formulas calculate correctly, it may be easier to directly type the references cells as opposed to use those that refer to GetPivotData.

The difference in rounding vs increase or decreasing decimals was demonstrated and the roundup function was used in the example. With increasing or decreasing decimals, the underlying decimal places still exist. While with rounding the decimal places are shortened to the specified values.

# Module 11

- Working with Data Sets: Date and Time
  - Date and Time Formatting
  - Join
  - Graphing with Secondary Axis
  - Scatterplot
  - Box and Whisker Plot
  - Analysis

Working with Time in Excel

Working with Time in Excel can be very helpful and powerful but also can be tricky. The phone call data set will be used to demonstrate a method to convert the date and times that we have for the calls in order to calculate the time between calls.

The data is sorted in Descending order by Date and then by time which is ideal for this example. If the date is not sorted in order the time between calculation will be incorrect.

| | Minutes | Date | Minute | AM PM |
|---|---|---|---|---|
| | 6 | 11/07/2023 | 06:14 | AM |
| | 4 | 11/06/2023 | 08:18 | PM |
| | 69 | 11/06/2023 | 07:10 | PM |
| 0 | 1 | 11/06/2023 | 07:06 | PM |
| 1 | 16 | 11/06/2023 | 06:39 | PM |
| 2 | 1 | 11/06/2023 | 05:35 | PM |
| 3 | 2 | 11/06/2023 | 02:13 | PM |
| 4 | 10 | 11/06/2023 | 11:22 | AM |
| 5 | 1 | 11/06/2023 | 11:11 | AM |
| 6 | 4 | 11/06/2023 | 11:04 | AM |

To Clean up the view for this example, 3 of the columns will be hidden.  Select entire columns of E, F, G and "Right Click" > Hide

| D | E | F | G | H | |
|---|---|---|---|---|---|
| | 0 | Count | | Search the menus | |
| | 209 | CountA | | ✂ Cut | |
| | 9 | Countifs | Std | 📋 Copy | |
| | 209 | Subtotal CountA | | 📋 Paste Options: | |
| | | | | 📋 🖼 | |
| 1 PM | **To** | **State** | **Ty** | | **Betv** |
| | Wife | SC | Call | Paste Special... | |
| | Wife | SC | Call | | |
| | Service | SC | Call | Insert | |
| | Restaurant | SC | Call | Delete | |
| | Wife | SC | Call | | |
| | Wife | SC | Call | Clear Contents | |
| | Store | Toll Free | Call | | |
| | Store | Toll Free | Call | Format Cells... | |
| | Toll Free | Toll Free | Call | | |
| | Toll Free | Toll Free | Call | Column Width... | |
| | Wife | SC | Call | | |
| | Store | Toll Free | Call | Hide | |
| | Toll Free | Toll Free | Call | Unhide | |
| | Friend | SC | Call | 11/06/2023 10:18 AM | |
| | Friend | SC | Call | 11/06/2023 10:16 AM | |
| | Wife | SC | Call | 11/06/2023 06:50 AM | |
| | Wife | SC | Call | 11/06/2023 05:39 AM | |
| | Brother | SC | Call | 11/05/2023 11:58 AM | |
| | Restaurant | SC | Call | 11/05/2023 10:22 AM | |
| | Restaurant | SC | Call | 11/04/2023 06:57 PM | |

Several columns will be used to transform the data and conduct the calculations and hiding is just cleaning up the view. The columns will be un-hidden when complete.

Also, a copy of the sheet was made by "Right Click" on the sheet name and Move or Copy > Create a Copy (check box).  The top rows with the subtotal formulas were deleted on the copy. The text data was also removed for this example, however, the same process would work for the time between text messages.

The 3 columns with date / time information are joined together using & and a space between them. This presented a format that Excel recognized as date / time.

Sometimes, getting the forma correct takes some trial and error. In this case it was tested by conducting the math and without the space it did not return a value so other attempts were made until it did.

| H2 | ▼ | ⋮ | ✕ | ✓ | fx | =B2&" "&C2&" "&D2 |

| | A | B | C | D | H |
|---|---|---|---|---|---|
| 1 | Minutes | Date | Minute | AM PM | Join with Space |
| 2 | 6 | 11/07/2023 | 06:14 | AM | 11/07/2023 06:14 AM |

This formula was copied down to all of the cells. The formulas and resulting values are shown below in the sample screen shot.

| H | I | J | K |
|---|---|---|---|
| Join with Space | Time Between Calls | Hours | Minutes |
| 11/07/2023 06:14 AM | =H2-H3 | =HOUR(I2) | =MINUTE(I2) |
| 11/06/2023 08:18 PM | 1:08:00 | 1 | 8 |
| 11/06/2023 07:10 PM | 0:04:00 | 0 | 4 |
| 11/06/2023 07:06 PM | 0:27:00 | 0 | 27 |
| 11/06/2023 06:39 PM | 1:04:00 | 1 | 4 |
| 11/06/2023 05:35 PM | 3:22:00 | 3 | 22 |
| 11/06/2023 02:13 PM | 2:51:00 | 2 | 51 |
| 11/06/2023 11:22 AM | 0:11:00 | 0 | 11 |
| 11/06/2023 11:11 AM | 0:07:00 | 0 | 7 |
| 11/06/2023 11:04 AM | 0:05:00 | 0 | 5 |
| 11/06/2023 10:59 AM | 0:03:00 | 0 | 3 |
| 11/06/2023 10:56 AM | 0:30:00 | 0 | 30 |
| 11/06/2023 10:26 AM | 0:08:00 | 0 | 8 |
| 11/06/2023 10:18 AM | 0:02:00 | 0 | 2 |

In order to prepare for a summary pivot table, the hours and minutes were combined by another formula to get total minutes. Results are shown below.

This is a great example of parenthesis use as we have to multiply the hours by 60 to convert to minutes before adding the other minutes.

| J | K | L |
|---|---|---|
| Hours | Minutes | Total Mintues |
| 9 | 56 | =(J2*60)+K2 |
| 1 | 8 | 68 |
| 0 | 4 | 4 |
| 0 | 27 | 27 |
| 1 | 4 | 64 |
| 3 | 22 | 202 |

Pivot Table and Analysis

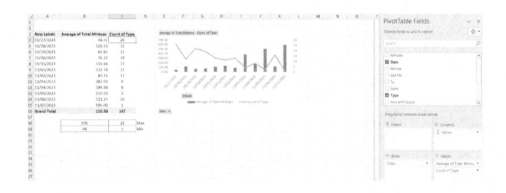

The Pivot Table is set up with the Date in Rows so we can see the average length between calls by day. Then in Values, there is Average of the time between call and the Count of Type gives us a count of the number of calls.

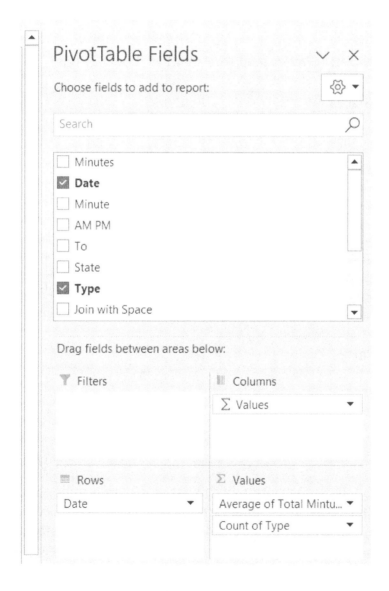

The resulting Pivot Table shows that overall the average time between calls is 203 minutes with an average of 12 calls per day.

These average numbers were obtained by highlighting the respective calls and checking the status bar for the various statistics.

| Row Labels ▾ | Average of Total Mintues | Count of Type |
|---|---|---|
| 10/27/2023 | 48.42 | 26 |
| 10/28/2023 | 120.33 | 12 |
| 10/29/2023 | 65.82 | 22 |
| 10/30/2023 | 76.32 | 19 |
| 10/31/2023 | 110.46 | 13 |
| 11/01/2023 | 132.18 | 11 |
| 11/02/2023 | 89.15 | 13 |
| 11/03/2023 | 382.00 | 4 |
| 11/04/2023 | 184.88 | 8 |
| 11/05/2023 | 510.50 | 2 |
| 11/06/2023 | 121.25 | 16 |
| 11/07/2023 | 596.00 | 1 |

Status Bar

Average: 203.11     Count: 12     Sum: 2437.31

We can visually see variation in the data for both number of calls and time between calls. Some formulas and some graphs can be used to help characterize and understand the process better.

Average, Min and Max Formulas

=Average()
=Min()
=Max()

These show the some days only had 1 call while others had 26.
The highest time between calls was 596 which is over 9 hours
while the lowest average time between calls was 48 minutes.

| Row Labels ▾ | Average of Total Mintues | Count of Type |
|---|---|---|
| 10/27/2023 | 48.42 | 26 |
| 10/28/2023 | 120.33 | 12 |
| 10/29/2023 | 65.82 | 22 |
| 10/30/2023 | 76.32 | 19 |
| 10/31/2023 | 110.46 | 13 |
| 11/01/2023 | 132.18 | 11 |
| 11/02/2023 | 89.15 | 13 |
| 11/03/2023 | 382.00 | 4 |
| 11/04/2023 | 184.88 | 8 |
| 11/05/2023 | 510.50 | 2 |
| 11/06/2023 | 121.25 | 16 |
| 11/07/2023 | 596.00 | 1 |

| | | |
|---|---|---|
| 596 | 26 | Max |
| 48 | 1 | Min |
| 203 | 12 | Average |

# Combination Line and Bar Graph: With a Secondary Axis

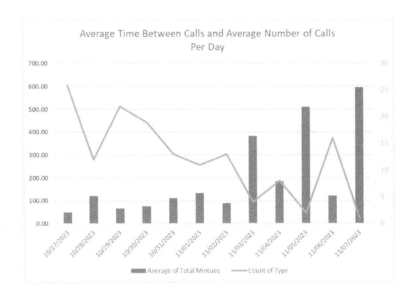

## Steps to get the combination graph with secondary axis are shown below.

# Combination Line and Bar Graph: With a Secondary Axis

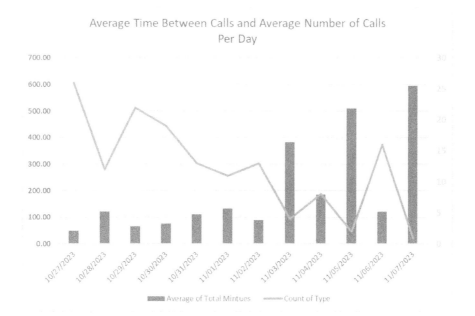

It can be really interesting and fun to utilize the data and visuals to analyze data and understand processes.

It looks like there are a few days with really high time between calls and some days have a lot more calls with low time between calls.

It turns out this scenario was an individual preparing for a home improvement project, thus making many calls then when working on the project in the later time frame was working solid and not making calls.

# Scatter Plot with Fitted Line

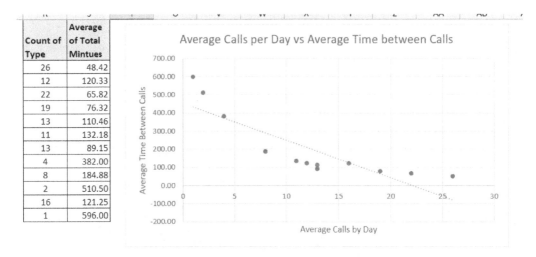

| Count of Type | Average of Total Mintues |
|---------------|--------------------------|
| 26 | 48.42 |
| 12 | 120.33 |
| 22 | 65.82 |
| 19 | 76.32 |
| 13 | 110.46 |
| 11 | 132.18 |
| 13 | 89.15 |
| 4 | 382.00 |
| 8 | 184.88 |
| 2 | 510.50 |
| 16 | 121.25 |
| 1 | 596.00 |

The Scatterplot confirms that the days with lower average calls has a higher time between calls and vice versa.

To create a scatter plot – Insert > Scatter
The line was added in Chart Design > Add Chart Element > Trendline > Linear

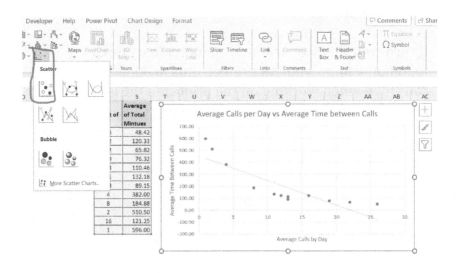

This slide shows a reference to scatterplots. Each single value is the intersection of the X and Y values for a given record.

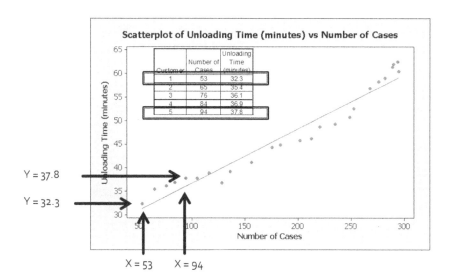

These can provide insight into the numbers that the eye cannot visually see in tables or other graph formats.

# Box and Whisker

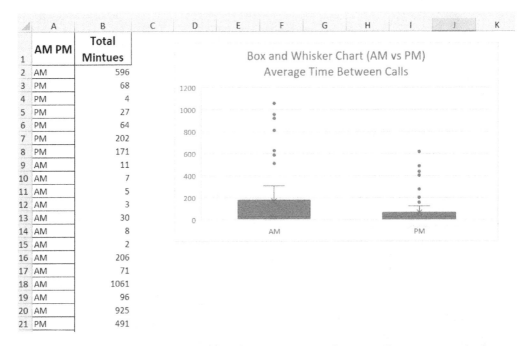

| | A | B |
|---|---|---|
| 1 | AM PM | Total Mintues |
| 2 | AM | 596 |
| 3 | PM | 68 |
| 4 | PM | 4 |
| 5 | PM | 27 |
| 6 | PM | 64 |
| 7 | PM | 202 |
| 8 | PM | 171 |
| 9 | AM | 11 |
| 10 | AM | 7 |
| 11 | AM | 5 |
| 12 | AM | 3 |
| 13 | AM | 30 |
| 14 | AM | 8 |
| 15 | AM | 2 |
| 16 | AM | 206 |
| 17 | AM | 71 |
| 18 | AM | 1061 |
| 19 | AM | 96 |
| 20 | AM | 925 |
| 21 | PM | 491 |

Highlight the Columns and Select Insert > Charts > Recommended then All Charts > Box and Whisker

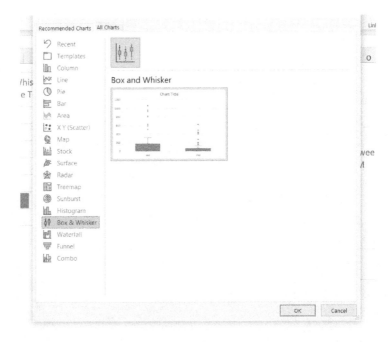

# Box and Whisker Compared to a Pivot Table Pivot Chart

| | Row Labels | Average of Total Mintues |
|---|---|---|
| | AM | 169.5 |
| | PM | 67.2 |
| | **Grand Total** | **110.3** |

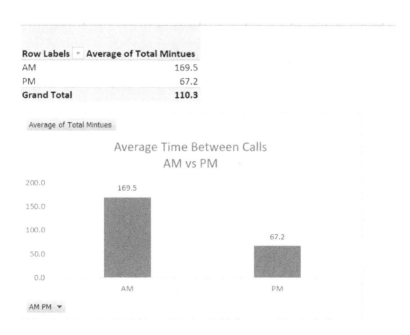

# Summary: Module 11

This module is another great application example that focusses on working with date and time. The join functionality using the & sign was used to combine the separate Date, Time, AM/PM together into an integrated date / time. Formulas were utilized to calculate the average time between calls.

Scatterplots and Box and Whisker plots were used to analyze the data for relationships. A combination bar and line chart with a secondary axis was used to depict data that was related but at different magnitude scales. The scatterplot is used for two sets of data that are continuous or numeric. Each plot on the scatterplot is the intersection of the two values at the same reference point. The Box and Whisker demonstration was comparing the average time between calls in the am and pm. The box and whisker is for a data combination that is categorical for one series and continuous or numeric for the other.

A quick pivot table bar chart made with the average time between calls by am and pm.

# Module 12

- Data Structure and Pivot Tables
- Keystrokes vs Scrolling
- VSTACK
- Power Query Pull
- VLOOKUP
- Conditional Formatting

# Module 12 – Pivot Tables Continued and Data Organization Methods

Module 12 will look at some different formats for data, input and organizing. We reviewed in an early lesson manual data entry from a handwritten sheet. Often the data is already in a spreadsheet form however it may need to be transformed to facilitate the analysis and use of pivot tables. Sometimes the layout that may look the best, may not be the best when it comes to flexibility with analysis. This example will look through a sample data set in different formats. As we work through these examples, we will build on the foundation that has been started and learn more features.

The scenario for the example is Quantity of Colored Beads by Date

### 1. All colors in same sheet with different columns

|   | A | B | C | D | E | F |
|---|---|---|---|---|---|---|
| 1 | Date | Blue | Red | Yellow | Green | |
| 2 | 1/1/2023 | 3 | 4 | 5 | 2 | |
| 3 | 1/2/2023 | 2 | 2 | 0 | 3 | |
| 4 | 1/3/2023 | 3 | 2 | 5 | 2 | |

### 2. All colors in same file and different sheets

|   | A | B | C |
|---|---|---|---|
|   | Date | Quantity | |
|   | 1/1/2023 | 3 | |
|   | 1/2/2023 | 2 | |
|   | 1/3/2023 | 3 | |

| Blue | Red | Yellow | Green |
|------|-----|--------|-------|

### 3. Colors are in different files

Pivot Table when data is in separate columns

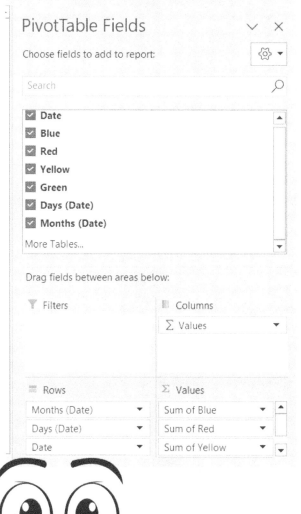

The colors can be total when there are entered into values separately.

This is called Un-stacked data and Pivot tables have increased flexibility when the data is Stacked. We will work on different methods to stack the data.

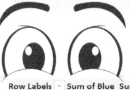

| Row Labels | Sum of Blue | Sum of Red | Sum of Yellow | Sum of Green |
|---|---|---|---|---|
| ⊞ Jan | 90 | 100 | 140 | 92 |
| ⊞ Feb | 69 | 79 | 121 | 85 |
| ⊞ Mar | 100 | 93 | 140 | 88 |
| ⊞ Apr | 102 | 86 | 117 | 87 |
| ⊞ May | 91 | 91 | 140 | 95 |
| ⊞ Jun | 78 | 90 | 128 | 97 |
| ⊞ Jul | 88 | 82 | 131 | 96 |
| ⊞ Aug | 97 | 97 | 121 | 96 |
| ⊞ Sep | 72 | 87 | 119 | 85 |
| ⊞ Oct | 97 | 97 | 117 | 90 |
| ⊞ Nov | 75 | 94 | 122 | 85 |
| ⊞ Dec | 74 | 97 | 124 | 86 |
| Grand Total | 1,033 | 1,094 | 1,519 | 1,081 |

Before moving forward with "stacking", notice how the date fields populated in the pivot table. They are "grouped" by month.

Let's take a look!

# Pivot Table date Grouping and Ungrouping

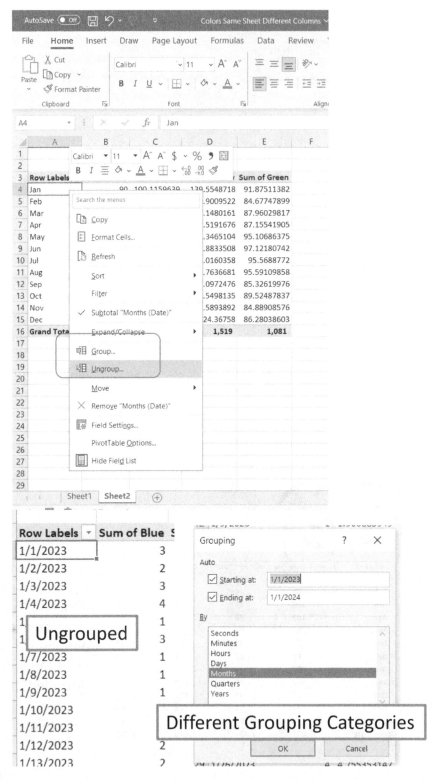

2. All colors in same file and different sheets

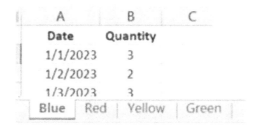

3. Colors are in different files

1. Label Color & Copy Paste
2. Label Color and Vstack formula
3. Utilize Power Query and Pull Data using formulas to pull color name

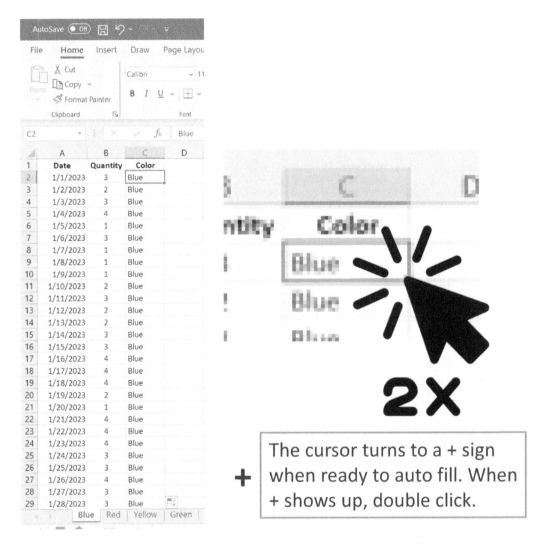

The cursor turns to a + sign when ready to auto fill. When + shows up, double click.

Create another column with Color, Type the color of the sheet and put the cursor in the bottom right corner and "Double Click" The Value typed in first cell will populate to the end of the data.

Repeat this for all Sheets – Auto Fill is a time saver.!

Module 12

# Manual Copy Paste

## Keystrokes to get to end of data quickly

Hold Shift Key

Click End then
Down Arrow
In a quick sequence

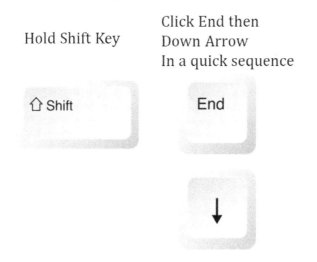

## Can also use scroll bar on the right and drag it to the bottom

# Vstack Formula

| | Date | Quantity | Color |
|---|---|---|---|
| 1. Copy Paste the Column Headers | | | |
| 2. Enter the formula =VSTACK(Blue:Green!A2:C5000) in cell C2) | 1/1/2023 | 3 | Blue |
| 3. Reformat Date Column to Short Date | 1/2/2023 | 2 | Blue |
| 4. The use of "5000" was arbitrary but used to extend beyond | 1/3/2023 | 3 | Blue |
| the data so the stacked column will continue to update. | 1/4/2023 | 4 | Blue |
| However, this creates 0's in column. Can use any end value | 1/5/2023 | 1 | Blue |
| beyond the total rows. | 1/6/2023 | 3 | Blue |
| | 1/7/2023 | 1 | Blue |
| 5. Add filter formula so final formula is | 1/8/2023 | 1 | Blue |
| =FILTER(VSTACK(Blue:Green!A2:C5000),VSTACK(Blue:Green!A2: | 1/9/2023 | 1 | Blue |
| A5000)<>0) this will actively filter out the 0's | 1/10/2023 | 2 | Blue |
| | 1/11/2023 | 3 | Blue |
| | 1/12/2023 | 2 | Blue |
| | 1/13/2023 | 2 | Blue |
| | 1/14/2023 | 3 | Blue |
| | 1/15/2023 | 3 | Blue |
| | 1/16/2023 | 4 | Blue |
| | 1/17/2023 | 4 | Blue |
| | 1/18/2023 | 4 | Blue |
| | 1/19/2023 | 2 | Blue |

# Power Query

A separate folder contains each of the files for the different colors.

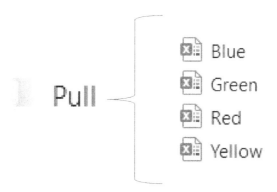

- Open a blank workbook and save it to a known place in the drive with the filename PowerQuery.

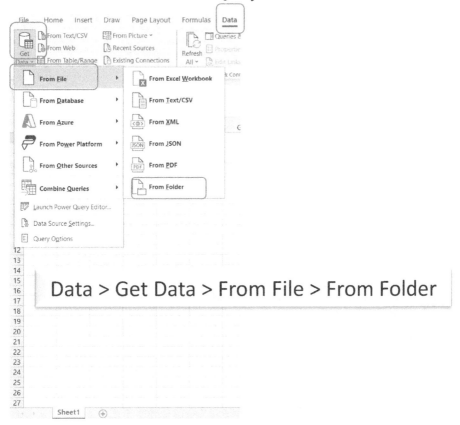

# Power Query

Combine Files

Select the object to be extracted from each file. Learn more

Sample File: First file

Display Options ▾

Parameter2 [1]
☐ Sheet1

Sheet1

| Date | Quantity |
|------|----------|
| 1/1/2023 | 3 |
| 1/2/2023 | 2 |
| 1/3/2023 | 3 |
| 1/4/2023 | 4 |
| 1/5/2023 | 1 |
| 1/6/2023 | 3 |
| 1/7/2023 | 1 |

## Select Sheet 1
## Preview the Data
## Click Ok

| | |
|------|---|
| 1/16/2023 | 4 |
| 1/17/2023 | 4 |
| 1/18/2023 | 4 |
| 1/19/2023 | 2 |
| 1/20/2023 | 1 |
| 1/21/2023 | 4 |

☐ Skip files with errors

OK

| | A | B | C |
|---|---|---|---|
| | Source.Name | Date | Quantity |
| | Blue.xlsx | 1/1/2023 | 3 |
| | Blue.xlsx | 1/2/2023 | 2 |
| | Blue.xlsx | 1/3/2023 | 3 |
| | Blue.xlsx | 1/4/2023 | 4 |
| | Blue.xlsx | 1/5/2023 | 1 |
| | Blue xlsx | 1/6/2023 | 3 |

## Check out the result!
- ### A new sheet Pull (the folder name) was created
- ### Column A is the Source File Name
- ### Columns B & C are the date & data columns

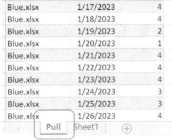

| Blue.xlsx | 1/17/2023 | 4 |
|-----------|-----------|---|
| Blue.xlsx | 1/18/2023 | 4 |
| Blue.xlsx | 1/19/2023 | 2 |
| Blue.xlsx | 1/20/2023 | 1 |
| Blue.xlsx | 1/21/2023 | 4 |
| Blue.xlsx | 1/22/2023 | 4 |
| Blue.xlsx | 1/23/2023 | 4 |
| Blue.xlsx | 1/24/2023 | 3 |
| Blue.xlsx | 1/25/2023 | 3 |
| Blue.xlsx | 1/26/2023 | 4 |

Pull   Sheet1   ⊕

# Power Query & Formulas: VLOOKUP

The VLOOKUP formula will be utilized to match the Region, Price and Leadtime information from the information table. As we step through the formula, think about how a person would perform this manually. Most likely it would be looking at the color on the main sheet and then cross referencing that to the information table entering it and repeating. The VLOOKUP formula can save a lot time and be used to combine different data sheets together

| Source.Name | Date | Quantity | Color | Length | If Statement | Region | Price | Leadtime |
|---|---|---|---|---|---|---|---|---|
| Blue.xlsx | 1/1/2023 | 3 Blu | | 9 | Blue | | | |
| Blue.xlsx | 1/2/2023 | 2 Blu | | 9 | Blue | | | |
| Blue.xlsx | 1/3/2023 | 3 Blu | | 9 | Blue | | | |
| Blue.xlsx | 1/4/2023 | 4 Blu | | 9 | Blue | | | |
| Blue.xlsx | 1/5/2023 | 1 Blu | | 9 | Blue | | | |
| Blue.xlsx | 1/6/2023 | 3 Blu | | 9 | Blue | | | |
| Blue.xlsx | 1/7/2023 | 1 Blu | | 9 | Blue | | | |
| Blue.xlsx | 1/8/2023 | 1 Blu | | 9 | Blue | | | |

| | 1 | 2 | 3 | 4 |
|---|---|---|---|---|
| | Color | Region | Price | Leadtime (Days) |
| | Red | North | 1 | 1 |
| | Yellow | South | 2.5 | 1 |
| | Blue | East | 3.15 | 3 |
| | Green | West | 4.25 | 5 |

Position in table where value is returned from

=VLOOKUP(F4, [Color Information Table.xlsx]Lookup'!$A$1:$D$5,2,FALSE)

False for Exact Match

Common field between both tables, used to match.

The file, sheet, and range of the data table where the match is made

## $A$1:$D$5, IMPORTANT

The $ ensure that the table range is always selected when the formula is copied down. When table is in the same workbook, these need to be manually entered.

# Power Query & Formulas: VLOOKUP

Excel has an integrated table functionality that when "formatted as a table" the formulas and formats autofill. It can be noticed in the example that the table that was created from the "pull" auto formatted as a live table. This allows for refresh of data when the folder is updated, as well. The formula structure is the same, however, instead of a cell value like F4, it refers to the column name with the @ symbol. It takes some getting used to but worth it as live tables can be powerful.

The vlookup formula below shows how it looks with the column references vs cell.

This format will be utilized for the remaining VLOOKUP's in the example.

=VLOOKUP([@[If Statement]],'[Color Information Table.xlsx]Lookup'!$A$1:$D$5,2,FALSE)

As the headers for year, month and week are added to the table, Excel autoformats the cells. After entering the headers, enter the formulas =Year(), =Month(), and =Weeknum() for the date field.

The Due Date can be calculated by adding the Date and Leadtime.

## Conditional Formatting

Conditional formatting will be added to the cell with the colors for practice.

# Conditional Formatting (Continued)

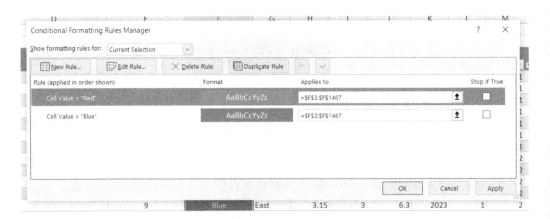

Continue added "New Rule" for each of the colors. Both fill and Text are being changed. The end result for all 4 colors would be below. Then hit ok.

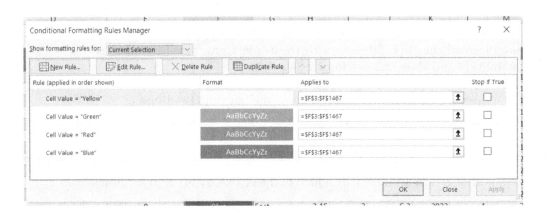

# Summary: Module 12

Module 12 works with handling different data formats. It demonstrates the advantages and disadvantages of organizing data in different ways. It shows an example of different color beads on the same sheet with different columns. The other version shows data in the same file but with colors on different sheets.

The stacked data method is an optimal choice when the plan is to use Pivot Tables. To get the data into the stacked format, a basic copy paste method can be used or the powerful VSTACK formula is also effective.

The power query was demonstrated on how it can be used to combine and load data from multiple spreadsheets easily into one source. This method creates a dynamic table that is able to be refreshed when new data is available in the folder and the formulas can autofill to new columns and rows.

Vlookup was used to pull information from a table with information unique to each color and multi level conditional formatting was used.

# Module 13

- Additional Techniques and Variations

Various Techniques

This module contains a combination of various techniques that are helpful in working with Microsoft Excel. Some of them are stand alone concept not covered in other parts of the course, while others are variations to a concept that was previously reviewed.

This section will help add additional functional to your tool kit and some of them will be used in more detail throughout the case studies. The items shown below are included within this section.

| |
|---|
| Working with Dates |
| Opening Multiple Files at Once |
| Multi-level Sorting |
| Conditional Formatting Multi Level |
| F4 Key and $ with Formula |
| Copy Paste Formats and Columns |
| Duplicates Identifying and Removing |
| Wingdings |
| Left, Mid, Right |
| Data Validation |
| Workiing with Time |
| Customize Ribbon |
| Password Protect |
| Paste into PowerPoint and PDF |
| Conditional Graphing |
| Spell Check and Translate |

## Working with Dates in Excel

Dates are stored as a serial number is Excel.  The serial number starts with 1/1/1900 being 1.  It can be seen in the screen shot below that serial numbers 1 and 2 are January 1 and January 2nd, 1900, respectively.  And the more recent date of November 1, 2023, has a serial number of 45231.

If a call is actually a date which would include Month, Day and Year, what shows up in the cell is dependent upon the formatting of the cell.

If the cell is formatted as a number, The serial number for the date will appear as a number, however, once a date format is chosen it will display for date indicators.

Regardless of the format, a date value in a cell will behave as a date. For example, if a calculation was being performed to get the difference between two days, it will calculate correctly because the underlying serial number is present.

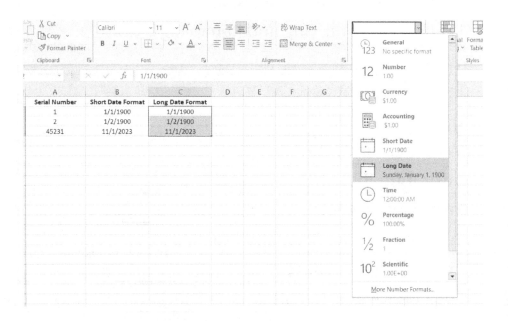

## Working with Dates in Excel

The menu below is obtained by clicking the Home Tab and then navigating to Format Cells and More Number formats and then the date category. There are many options for date formatting and also allows for Locale changes.

While the formatting in a particular cell can change, for example, only the month and year may be visible as in Nov-23 or 11/23, keep in mind that the full date serial number is underlying which includes month, day, and year.

| Serial Number | Short Date Format | Long Date Format |
|---|---|---|
| 1 | 1/1/1900 | Sunday, January 1, 1900 |
| 2 | 1/2/1900 | Monday, January 2, 1900 |
| 45231 | 11/1/2023 | Wednesday, November 1, 2023 |
| 45232 | 11/2/2023 | Thursday, November 2, 2023 |
| | | |
| 1 | 1 | 1 |
| =A5-A4 | =B5-B4 | =C5-C4 |

## Opening Multiple Files

Helpful Tip: If there are multiple files in a folder that you would like to open all at once. It is possible to select up to 16 at one time and then "Right Click" and choose open. They will each open in a new window.

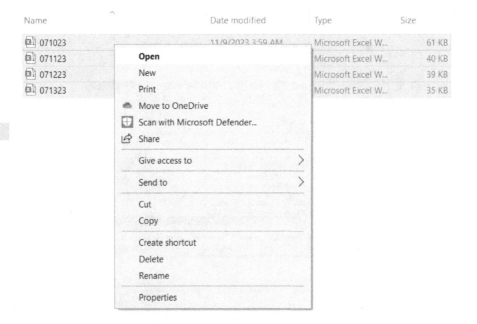

This is not necessarily a Microsoft Excel feature; however, it can come in very handy in the instance where there are several files that are going to be opened. This can represent a time savings.

## Multi Level Sorting

The file used in this example is the completed bead order file where the state was separated out from the address using Text to Columns functionality.

This example will show how to sort using multiple criteria. Click Data > Sort and select the sort icon.

Sort

Below shows the settings for sorting the orders by State first, then by Due Date and then by Last Name.

The sort menu can be used to Add or Delete levels as well as rearrange them.

This feature gives added flexibility with organizing the data

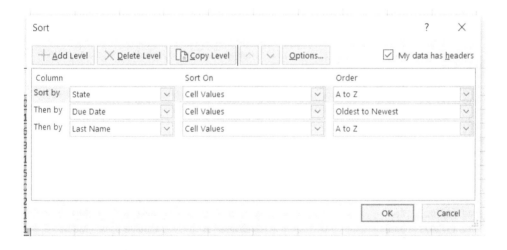

The resulting table is on the next page.

## Multi Level Sorting

The table below shows the results of the three-level sort that was conducted based on the settings on the prior page. It can be seen that the state field is sorted first and where there are multiple state entries the date will be in order for those entries and the same is true for the last name. When there are repeats of the same date for a given state the fields are in order by last name.

| Order Number | Due Date | Color | Quantity | Last Name | First Name | State | Zip |
|---|---|---|---|---|---|---|---|
| 1012 | 12/1/2023 | Yellow | 19 | Ellis | Billy | AR | 71730 |
| 1035 | 12/9/2023 | Yellow | 20 | Cruz | Isiah | AZ | 85351 |
| 1010 | 12/6/2023 | Green | 10 | Jenkins | Sabrina | CT | 6606 |
| 1048 | 12/8/2023 | Green | 10 | Mendez | Holly | FL | 32043 |
| 1039 | 12/18/2023 | Green | 6 | Bradley | Kamari | FL | 34231 |
| 1028 | 12/18/2023 | Red | 15 | Mcgee | Shamar | FL | 32955 |
| 1049 | 12/24/2023 | Blue | 18 | Heath | Keyon | FL | 33010 |
| 1047 | 12/9/2023 | Red | 11 | Huang | Jude | IA | 50322 |
| 1007 | 12/30/2023 | Green | 6 | Mcconnell | Shawn | IA | 51501 |
| 1022 | 12/10/2023 | Yellow | 14 | Williamson | Zack | IL | 60411 |
| 1017 | 12/24/2023 | Green | 1 | Caldwell | Ellis | IL | 60402 |
| 1018 | 12/30/2023 | Green | 12 | Donovan | Meadow | IL | 60007 |
| 1027 | 12/30/2023 | Red | 7 | Wilcox | Nathan | IL | 60201 |
| 1029 | 12/15/2023 | Red | 16 | Huynh | Nathanial | IN | 47130 |
| 1040 | 12/19/2023 | Yellow | 5 | Bender | Sonia | MA | 1420 |
| 1032 | 12/1/2023 | Red | 12 | Bartlett | Chance | MD | 21114 |
| 1004 | 12/9/2023 | Blue | 12 | Swanson | Carmen | MD | 21222 |
| 1013 | 12/10/2023 | Red | 17 | Mccann | Juliana | MD | 21208 |
| 1011 | 12/15/2023 | Blue | 14 | Weaver | Camille | MD | 21030 |
| 1045 | 12/18/2023 | Red | 12 | Howell | Arnav | MD | 20744 |
| 1050 | 12/30/2023 | Yellow | 17 | Smith | Jorge | MD | 20746 |

## Conditional Formatting – Multi Level and Stop if True

Filename: Orders – sheet Stop if True is hidden, unhide to view

The table below is showing the result of conditional formatting that is based on comparing the value of the leads to the goal and then coloring the entire row vs just the value.

The steps to perform this will apply conditional formatting rules for the order, stop if true check box as well as absolute and relative references. Absolute and Relative references are the $ signs in the cell address reference to freeze the values.

| Month | Leads | Goal | Meet Goal | Smile? |
|-------|-------|------|-----------|--------|
| Jan | 100 | 150 | No | ☹ |
| Feb | 125 | 150 | No | ☹ |
| Mar | 118 | 150 | No | ☹ |
| Apr | 130 | 150 | No | ☹ |
| May | 132 | 150 | No | ☹ |
| Jun | 140 | 150 | No | ☹ |
| Jul | 150 | 150 | Yes | ☺ |
| Aug | 145 | 150 | No | ☹ |
| Sep | 160 | 150 | Yes | ☺ |
| Oct | | 150 | No | ☹ |
| Nov | | 150 | No | ☹ |
| Dec | | 150 | No | ☹ |

# Screen Shots: for Conditional Formatting Steps

| Month | Leads | Goal | Meet Goal | Smile? |
|-------|-------|------|-----------|--------|
| Jan | 100 | 150 | Yes | ☺ |
| Feb | 125 | 150 | Yes | ☺ |
| Mar | 118 | 150 | Yes | ☺ |
| Apr | 130 | 150 | Yes | ☺ |
| May | 132 | 150 | Yes | ☺ |
| Jun | 140 | 150 | Yes | ☺ |
| Jul | 150 | 150 | Yes | ☺ |
| Aug | 145 | 150 | Yes | ☺ |
| Sep | 160 | 150 | No | ☹ |
| Oct |  | 150 | Yes | ☺ |
| Nov |  | 150 | Yes | ☺ |
| Dec |  | 150 | Yes | ☺ |

**New Formatting Rule**  ? × 

Select a Rule Type:

- ► Format all cells based on their values
- ► Format only cells that contain
- ► Format only top or bottom ranked values
- ► Format only values that are above or below average
- ► Format only unique or duplicate values
- ► Use a formula to determine which cells to format

Edit the Rule Description:

Format values where this formula is true:

=$B$2>=$C$2

Preview:  AaBbCcYyZz  Format...

OK  Cancel

# Format values where this formula is true:

## =$B$2>=$C$2

### Formula: =$B2=""

### Formula: =$B2<$C2

Format Painter will be used to copy this format to the other rows. Since the columns won't change but the rows will, the $ were adjusted.

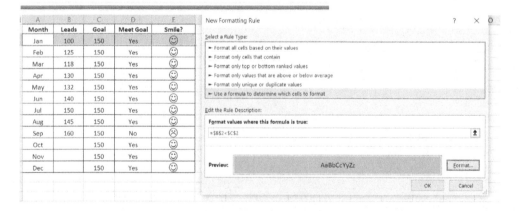

| Month | Leads | Goal | Meet Goal | Smile? |
|-------|-------|------|-----------|--------|
| Jan | 100 | 150 | Yes | ☺ |
| Feb | 125 | 150 | Yes | ☺ |
| Mar | 118 | 150 | Yes | ☺ |
| Apr | 130 | 150 | Yes | ☺ |
| May | 132 | 150 | Yes | ☺ |
| Jun | 140 | 150 | Yes | ☺ |
| Jul | 150 | 150 | Yes | ☺ |
| Aug | 145 | 150 | Yes | ☺ |
| Sep | 160 | 150 | No | ☹ |
| Oct |  | 150 | Yes | ☺ |
| Nov |  | 150 | Yes | ☺ |
| Dec |  | 150 | Yes | ☺ |

**New Formatting Rule**  ? × 

Select a Rule Type:

- ► Format all cells based on their values
- ► Format only cells that contain
- ► Format only top or bottom ranked values
- ► Format only values that are above or below average
- ► Format only unique or duplicate values
- ► Use a formula to determine which cells to format

Edit the Rule Description:

Format values where this formula is true:

=$B$2<$C$2

Preview:  AaBbCcYyZz  Format...

OK  Cancel

## Screen Shots: for Conditional Formatting Steps

The format was created for row 2, the $ references were adjusted, and the format painter was used to transfer the formatting to the remaining rows. This is why it shows repeating in the window. The first group is the original formatting on one row only and the second is where it is painted to multiple. The applied to rows could be changed to include all, however, this view was left for examples purposes because this is a realistic way conditional formatting could look.

The other really important aspect is the stop if true checkbox on the white. If that were not checked then even though it is true that the cell is blank and would be white, it is also true that the blank cell is less than 150 so since the red format is after the white, it would result in the red. The stop if true avoids this.

Also, there are arrows where the order of the conditions can be changed to facilitate the process.

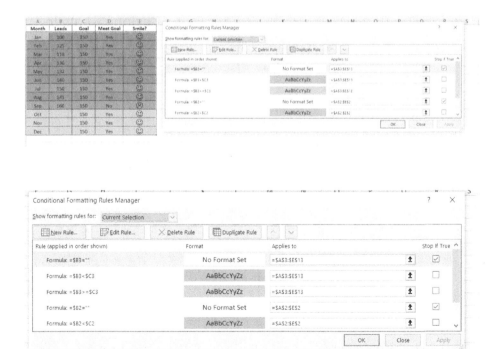

**F4 Key** – the F4 key can be used to enter the $ for absolute and relative cell references or freezing.

Below shows a simple formula that adds cell A1 to cell A2.  The first example has no freezing in place.

By highlighting the cells as shown and Clicking F4 key on the keyboard the $ signs will cycle through in the order shown

=SUM(A1:A2)

=SUM($A$1:$A$2)

F4 One Time: Puts All $ on columns and rows

=SUM(A$1:A$2)

Clicking F4 again, removes the $ from Column and leaves on Rows

=SUM($A1:$A2)

Clicking F4 again, removes the $ from Row and leaves on Column

=SUM(A1:A2)

Clicking F4 again, removes all of the $

This is a helpful keystroke that facilities putting the $ on formulas.  The $ can also be put on manually.

## Copy – Paste – Formats and Column Widths

Within the Paste Menu – there are two options that will allow for copying of column widths and formats.

| Date | Red | Blue | Green | Yellow |
|---|---|---|---|---|
| 1/1 | 5 | 4 | 1 | 1 |
| 1/5 | 4 | 3 | 1 | 2 |
| 1/10 | 10 | 1 | 1 | 3 |
| 1/12 | 5 | 2 | 2 | 1 |
| 1/15 | 2 | 3 | 3 | 3 |

| Date | Red | Blue | Green | Yellow |
|---|---|---|---|---|
| 45292 | 5 | 4 | 1 | 1 |
| 45296 | 4 | 3 | 1 | 2 |
| 45301 | 10 | 1 | 1 | 3 |
| 45303 | 5 | 2 | 2 | 1 |
| 45306 | 2 | 3 | 3 | 3 |

The table to the left shows the result of Copy > Paste > Values of the data table above.

Selecting the options highlighted allow for copying of formats and column widths. The results are shown in the visuals below.

| Date | Red | Blue | Green | Yellow |
|---|---|---|---|---|
| 1/1 | 5 | 4 | 1 | 1 |
| 1/5 | 4 | 3 | 1 | 2 |
| 1/10 | 10 | 1 | 1 | 3 |
| 1/12 | 5 | 2 | 2 | 1 |
| 1/15 | 2 | 3 | 3 | 3 |

### Duplicates: Identifying and Removing
File: Orders for Duplicates

Having duplicate records in a data set can be troublesome as it can cause inaccurate totals and summaries.

This example will go through the steps of identifying duplicates using conditional formatting and removing them using one of Excel's data tools. Filter on cells color or value can also help view the duplicates after the format is placed on.

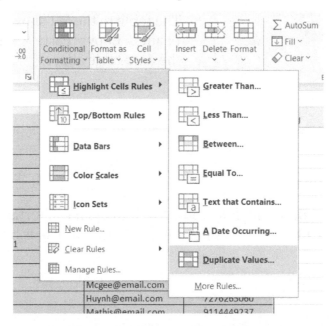

The steps to highlight duplicate values are in Home > Conditional Formatting > Highlight Cell Rules > Duplicate Values

| Order Number | Due Date | Color |
|---|---|---|
| 1001 | 12/1/2023 | Blue |
| 1002 | 12/10/2023 | Green |
| 1003 | 12/5/2023 | Yellow |
| 1004 | 12/9/2023 | Blue |
| 1005 | 12/8/2023 | Blue |
| 1006 | 12/24/2023 | Blue |
| 1007 | 12/30/2023 | Green |
| 1008 | 12/18/2023 | Yellow |
| 1009 | 12/15/2023 | Red |
| 1028 | 12/18/2023 | Red |
| 1029 | 12/15/2023 | Red |
| 1030 | 12/6/2023 | Green |
| 1031 | 12/15/2023 | Yellow |
| 1032 | 12/1/2023 | Red |
| 1033 | 12/10/2023 | Green |
| 1034 | 12/5/2023 | Blue |
| 1010 | 12/6/2023 | Green |

The highlighted cells shows the duplicates

## Duplicates: Identifying and Removing

It is possible to "Right Click" and filter on the value or cell color. Once the cell color filter is in place, the entire row can be removed using right click delete. This will remove the entire row when the row number is selected prior to deleting.

The table below shows the result of the "right click" filter on cell value.

| Order Number | Due Date | Color | Quantity | Last Name | First Name | Address | Email | Phone Number |
|---|---|---|---|---|---|---|---|---|
| 1004 | 12/9/2023 | Blue | 12 | Swanson | Carmen | 203 1st St. Dundalk, MD 21222 | Swanson@email.com | 6434506414 |
| 1004 | 12/9/2023 | Blue | 12 | Swanson | Carmen | 203 1st St. Dundalk, MD 21222 | Swanson@email.com | 6434506414 |

Using the "Right Click" filter on cells color can be used to identify all of the duplicates in order to review.

## Duplicates: Identifying and Removing

In the Data Tab under Data Tools there is an icon with the process to remove duplicates.

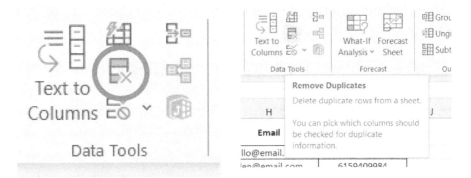

The tool defaults to header rows and has all columns selected. Click > Unselect All and then, for this example, click Order Number

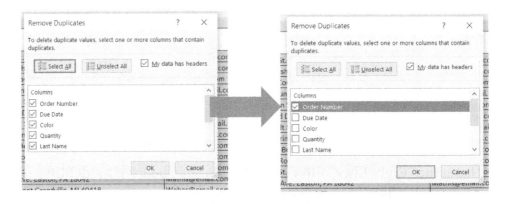

After clicking Ok, a message box shows up indicating how many duplicates were removed and how many remain. This is a good way to do a logical verification if the numbers seem correct. If the result doesn't seem to align with what would be expected, the undo button can be used to return the values and verify.

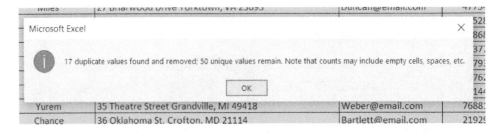

# Wingdings

The table below shows a reference for the four fonts, Wingdings, Wingdings 2, Wingdings, 3 and Webdings.

These can be used within spreadsheet cells and gives some simple options to create visualizations.

| | a | b | c | d | e | f | g | h | i | j | k | l | m | n | o | p | q | r | s | t | u | v | w | x | y | z |
|---|---|---|---|---|---|---|---|---|---|---|---|---|---|---|---|---|---|---|---|---|---|---|---|---|---|---|
| Wingdings | | | | | | | | | | | | | | | | | | | | | | | | | | |
| Wingdings 2 | | | | | | | | | | | | | | | | | | | | | | | | | | |
| Wingdings 3 | | | | | | | | | | | | | | | | | | | | | | | | | | |
| Webdings | | | | | | | | | | | | | | | | | | | | | | | | | | |

| | A | B | C | D | E | F | G | H | I | J | K | L | M | N | O | P | Q | R | S | T | U | V | W | X | Y | Z |
|---|---|---|---|---|---|---|---|---|---|---|---|---|---|---|---|---|---|---|---|---|---|---|---|---|---|---|---|
| Wingdings | | | | | | | | | | | | | | | | | | | | | | | | | | |
| Wingdings 2 | | | | | | | | | | | | | | | | | | | | | | | | | | |
| Wingdings 3 | | | | | | | | | | | | | | | | | | | | | | | | | | |
| Webdings | | | | | | | | | | | | | | | | | | | | | | | | | | |

| | 1 | 2 | 3 | 4 | 5 | 6 | 7 | 8 | 9 | 10 | 11 | 12 | 13 | 14 | 15 | 16 | 17 | 18 | 19 | 20 | 21 | 22 | 23 | 24 | 25 | 26 |
|---|---|---|---|---|---|---|---|---|---|---|---|---|---|---|---|---|---|---|---|---|---|---|---|---|---|---|---|
| Wingdings | | | | | | | | | | | | | | | | | | | | | | | | | | |
| Wingdings 2 | | | | | | | | | | | | | | | | | | | | | | | | | | |
| Wingdings 3 | | | | | | | | | | | | | | | | | | | | | | | | | | |
| Webdings | | | | | | | | | | | | | | | | | | | | | | | | | | |

## Left, Mid, Right

Left, Mid, and Right formulas can be used to extract values for within the cell. They can be used alone or in combination.

The table below shows an example of pulling out the different parts of a phone number.

The formula is shown in the first row and the resulting values in the remaining rows.

| Phone Number | First 3 | Middle 3 | Last For |
|---|---|---|---|
| (639) 942-6414 | =LEFT(A2,3) | =MID(A2,4,3) | =RIGHT(A2,4) |
| (615) 940-9984 | 615 | 940 | 9984 |
| (707) 822-4701 | 707 | 822 | 4701 |
| (643) 450-6414 | 643 | 450 | 6414 |

Len

The Len formula will return the number of characters within a cell. This can be used distinguish different values or in conjunction with other formulas.

## Data Validation

The Data Validation tool has multiple uses.  The first example will show how it can be used to error proof entry into a cell.

Data Validation > Settings > Whole Number is used for the example and an acceptable range between 1 and 10.

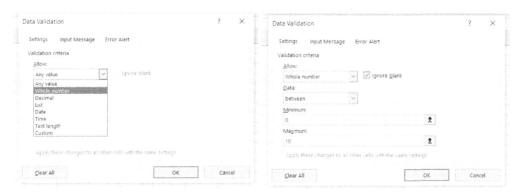

Clicking on a value outside that range will prompt the error message. There are other criteria options such as date, time, text, length and others that can be specified.

Use of Data Validation in this manner  can be a helpful aid for data entry.

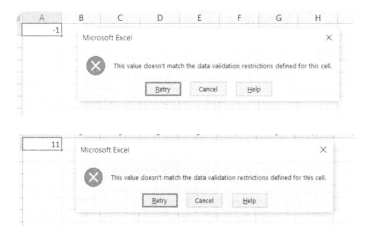

### Data Validation

The Data Validation tool with the List selection can be used to create a drop-down menu within a cell.

Once the list selection is made, the source or entries within the drop down need to be specified. This can be done by either typing the options directly into the source box separating each option with a comma or by reference a source range.

The drop downs are popular for data entry. They can help save time with typing and also ensure that each entry of like types is spelled in the same way.

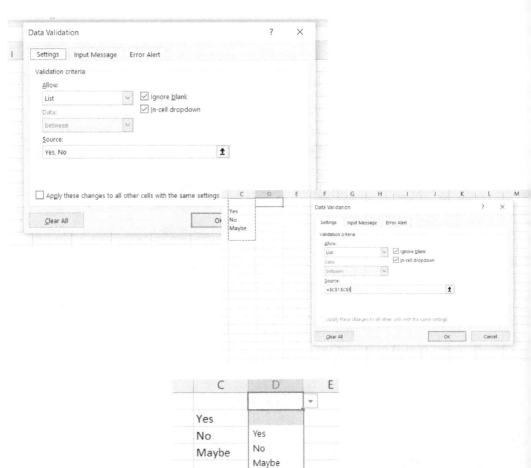

## Data Validation

Within the data validation menu, it is possible to customize the error alert message.

The error message can also be turned off.  This would allow entry of any value into the cell in combination with use of the drop down.

There is an Input Message functionality, as well. That will prompt a message when the cell is clicked.

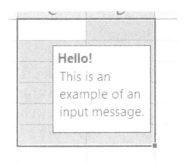

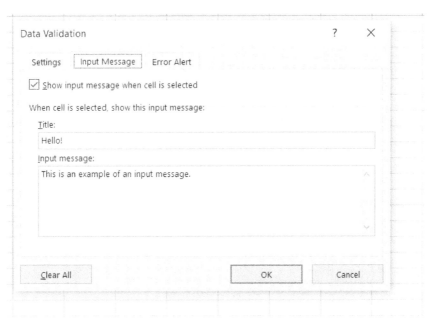

## Time in Excel

Excel stores time in cell values as a serial number. This is a similar concept to the serial number used in dates. To gain a frame of reference, 12:00 AM is hour 0 and 1 hour represents 1/24 of a day. The decimal value for 1 hour is 1/24 = .041666. Formatting and converting dates to the desired units can be accomplished.

Below shows some examples. The first example, shows the difference which is 1 hour and 5 minutes, formatted as a time does not provide a useful representation. However, it can be formatted using the time format highlighted and it will show the hours, minutes and seconds of the difference.

Mathematical conversions can also be used to calculate differences. Hours and Minutes formulas are shown below for this example. To Convert the difference between two times in hours the formula is the difference * 24, for minutes it is *1440 and for seconds it is * 86400.

| Time | Time | Difference |
|------|------|------------|
| 8:30 AM | 9:30 AM | 1:00 AM |
| 8:30 AM | 8:35 AM | 12:05 AM |

| Time | Time | Difference | Difference Minute | Difference Hour | | |
|------|------|------------|-------------------|-----------------|---|---|
| 8:30 AM | 9:30 AM | 1:00:00 | 60 | 1 | =C7*1440 | =C7*24 |
| 8:30 AM | 8:35 AM | 0:05:00 | 5 | 0.0833 | =C8*1440 | =C8*24 |

| Time | Time | Difference |
|------|------|------------|
| 8:30 AM | 9:30 AM | 0.0416667 |
| 8:30 AM | 8:35 AM | 0.0034722 |

# Customize ribbon

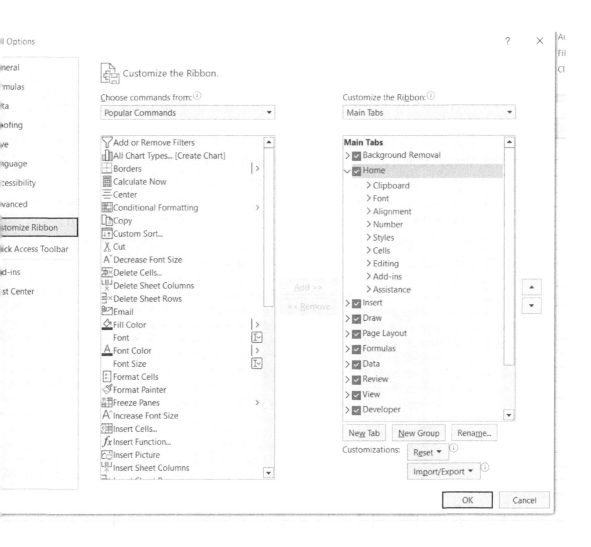

## Password Protect

There are different types of password protection and security options. One is protecting the entire file either as read only or by requiring a password to open.

The other type is protecting specific sheets and or cells within sheets. This option requires indicating which cells will be locked and unlocked when the sheet is protected.

The file protection option is located in File > Info and is called Protect Workbook.

The Always Open as Read Only option is great for protecting the file from unwanted changes while allowing anyone with the file to open it and review but just not make changes. The individual could save a copy of the file after opening in read only, but the original file will remain the same upon closing. The read only option will prompt a message upon opening indicating that the file is read only.

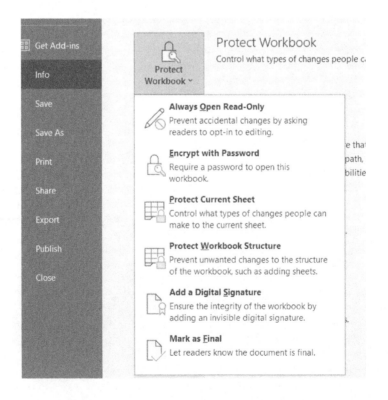

## Password Protect

Encrypt with password allows for setting a password and making it required upon opening the file. This is located in Encrypt with Password.

It is important to take note of the message provided by Microsoft Excel in that passwords are case sensitive and once put on the file can not be recovered in other ways.  The user must remember or know the passwords.

This option is a good choice when control is desired around access to the information inside the file. This common for sensitive or confidential information.

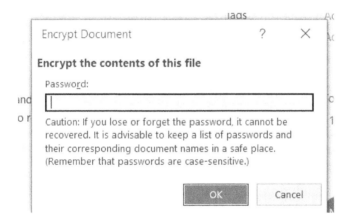

## Password Protect

The next type of protection that will be reviewed is protecting the worksheet or some of the content within the worksheet. This feature is located in the Review Tab Menu and the option to protect a sheet.

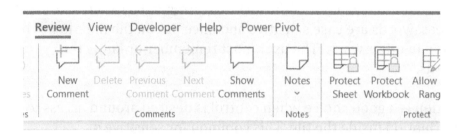

There are several options for different combinations of protection, for example, formatting and editing can be protected or just one or the other. There are options to allow Pivot Tables to be interacted with by the user.

This introduction will provide the basis on selecting the cells to be protected and protecting the sheet.

By default, within protection every cell is set to be locked when the sheet protection is on. To access the cell protection setting, click on a cell or a range of cells and right click. Go to format cells and when the window opens click on protection. It is within this menu that the setting exists to set it as locked or not.

## Password Protect

The example shows two sets of cells, one has the checkbox locked checked and the other does not, indicated by unlocked. Then the Protect Sheet icon is checked.

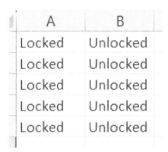

Protect
Sheet W

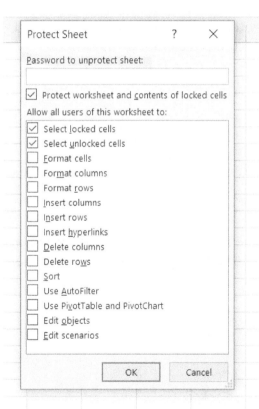

A window will pop up with the preferences for what is allowed. By default, only selecting cells is allowed.

This option allows for including a password or not.

**Password Protect**

Once the Protect Sheet icon has been selected, the icon will change to show "Unprotect Sheet". This is a good indicator that protection is on the sheet. Sometimes a file is received that has protected cells and it is not obvious upon opening. Taking a look at this section within the Review menu will confirm if protection is set.

Upon trying to edit or type in a protected cell the message below will pop up. This indicates that the selected cell cannot be modified.

The cells that were not locked in the format cells protection option, are able to be edited as seen below. The work Type was entered into that cell.

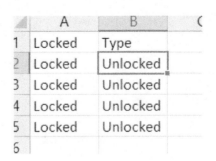

| | A | B | C |
|---|---|---|---|
| 1 | Locked | Type | |
| 2 | Locked | Unlocked | |
| 3 | Locked | Unlocked | |
| 4 | Locked | Unlocked | |
| 5 | Locked | Unlocked | |
| 6 | | | |

## Password Protect

It is important to note that protecting the sheet with the default selections also removes the ability to format the sheet or change any columns or rows.

This can be seen below as the Home and Insert Menus are grayed out.

This is another indicator that worksheet protection has been enabled.

As the default is to lock all of the cells, it is sometimes an easier approach to select the entire sheet and unlock every cell. Then only select the desired cells for locking and format those as such.

Clicking in the far-right corner, selects every cell on the entire sheet. At that point Right Click > Format Cells can be selected, and the protection tab can be entered and uncheck the locked checkbox.

Then you can go in and select the cells or range of cells and mark them as locked,

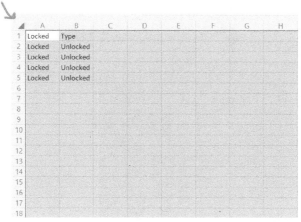

**Password Protect**

To remove the worksheet protection, just click again on the Unprotect worksheet. If there is no password, it will release the cells and formatting immediately. If there is a password the password has to be successfully entered prior to the unlocking to take place.

**Version History and Manage Workbook**

Two other helpful features within the Info menu are version history and Manage workbook. These can help recover and earlier version or any versions with unsaved changes.

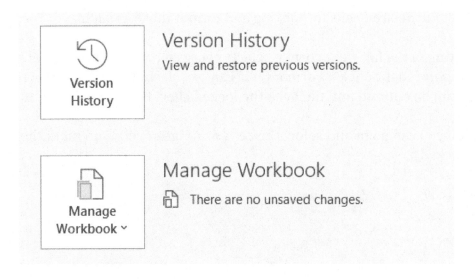

## Paste Into PowerPoint and Saving as PDF

Copying and pasting spreadsheet information and charts into a PowerPoint can be useful for presentations or for sharing a graph package. There are different pasting options.

Pasting as an Enhanced Metafile helps with resizing and formatting the result. This is great for graphs or sections of tables that are going to be shared in a presentation.

The paste link option which is demonstrated in detail in the Module 15 case study keeps selection live back to the Microsoft Excel sheet and can be updated when new data is available in the worksheet.

Below shows the menu options.

This is another good area to practice with the different options to explore what is best for your application.

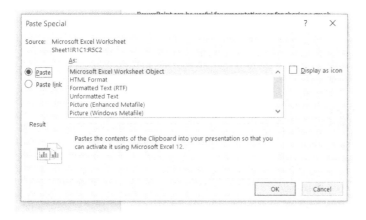

Another technique commonly used for sharing of graph packages is putting the information into a PowerPoint slide presentation and then saving that presentation as a PDF file. This can be found within PowerPoint's save options.

## Conditional Graphs - Red Green Example

While conditional formatting is an available and helpful option for cell contents, it is not directly available for graphs.

A method demonstrated in the dashboarding module showed how multiple series are created with conditions and then those series can be graphed and set to their own unique colors. As the data changes, the if statements will populate that series and update the chart respectively. The example, was created with two series and using the colors of red and green but this can be expanded to more than two series and any color choices.

The set up for this style graph with two series and IF statements are shown below.

| Week | Staffing Target | Staffing Level | Meet Goal | Not Meet Goal |
|---|---|---|---|---|
| Week 1 | 100 | 90 | =IF(C2>=B2,C2,"") | =IF(C2<B2,C2,"") |
| Week 2 | 100 | 95 | | 95 |
| Week 3 | 100 | 100 | 100 | |
| Week 4 | 100 | 99 | | 99 |
| Week 5 | 100 | 98 | | 98 |
| Week 6 | 100 | 101 | 101 | |
| Week 7 | 100 | 100 | 100 | |
| Week 8 | 100 | 100 | 100 | |
| Week 9 | 100 | 99 | | 99 |
| Week 10 | 100 | 98 | | 98 |
| Week 11 | 100 | 97 | | 97 |
| Week 12 | 100 | 100 | 100 | |

## Time Stamp

At times, it is desired to put a timestamp into a cell when another cell is populated. The formula below will perform this. Just the cell references need to be updated for the sheet desired. This formula puts the timestamp in F3 when E3 is populated. To change just modify the cell references of E3 and F3.

`=IF(E3<>"",IF(F3="",NOW(),F3),"")`

There is one other detail that needs to be changed to make this work. In File > Options > Formulas
Check the box Enable Iterative calculations and increase the maximum to 10000.

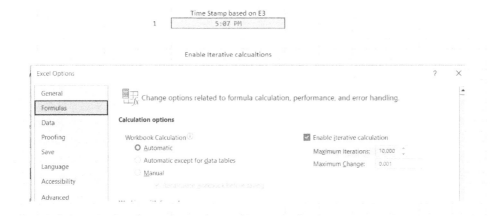

## Spell Check and Translate

Within the review tab, there are two features to highlight as the usage is common. The Spelling tab will perform a spell check within each cell. This is helpful to ensure that little typos did not create incorrect spelling of words.

There is also a translate option where words or phrases can be entered and then a copy to clipboard option can be utilized to paste it back into the spreadsheet.

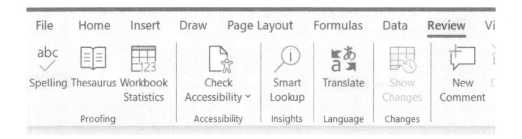

# Summary: Module 13

This module provided an array of different functionality that can be used in conjunction with other techniques to effectively create and utilize Microsoft Excel. While there are many options available within the program, this section featured a few that are commonly used and helpful. Many of them time to the case studies that will be reviewed in the later modules.

Please take note that this list is not inclusive but rather a selection of helpful techniques.

# Module 14

- Visual Basic Application Macros

Macros are programs that are used to automate steps and operations. It can help save time, reduce errors, improve functionality and enhance the user experience. Microsoft Excel using Visual Basic Application (VBA) programming language to create macros. In this module, we will learn how to get started with VBA and implement some macros in spreadsheets.

When a spreadsheet has a macro, it needs to be saved as macro enabled which is within the saving options for file type.

Macros are great, however, there are some risks associated with macros from unknown sources and many systems and network are set up to protect users by disabling macros. If a file has macros that are not enabled and will not run, the trust center settings can be changed for those where the source is trusted.

Prior to changing trust center settings, ensure that you know and trust the source of the document. In order to enable and trust, Select File > Options. Select Trust Center, then click Trust Center Settings... Select Trusted Locations. Enter the path to location. You can also trust specific files. In some cases, when the file is opened, it will give a message asking if you want to enable macros and there will be an option to do so.

To get started Open a blank workbook and go to File > Save As and change the file type to macro enabled. Give the file the name macro.

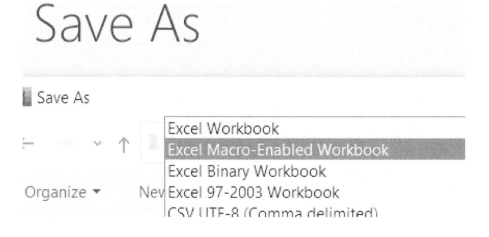

We will start getting acclimated to macros by recording some basic steps and reviewing the code that Microsoft Excel created.

Go to View > Macro > Record Macro
Enter Name – first

For the steps click in cell A1 then go to C5 and type this is my first macro! And go to Macro and hit stop recording.

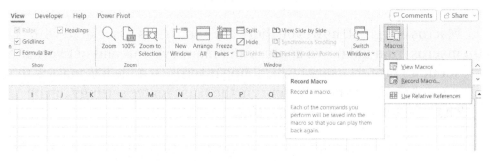

Now, go to View > Macros > View macros

Select the one named "first" and click edit.

The window that opens is called the Visual Basic Editor and the script for the steps performed are below. As you record small steps and review the code, you can start learning the language and convention.

```
Sub first()
'
' first Macro
'


'
    Range("C5").Select
    ActiveCell.FormulaR1C1 = "This is my first macro!"
    Range("C6").Select
End Sub
```

The visual basic editor is below:

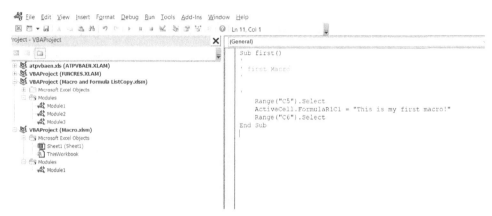

In this window, there is a section that shows the workbook structure and all sheets. Some macros go on the worksheet, some on workbook and others go into modules. It can be seen that Module 1 was created when we made this first macro.

Macros begin with Sub then the name and () and will always end with End Sub.

For troubleshooting purposes or if there is a part of the code that you don't want included, if a single quote ' is put it front, it will turn that code into text and will not execute it. The color also changes to green so it can be noticed that it is text.

It is a good practice to put text notes inside of the longer macros to explain what the code is doing or to give instructions regarding the macro.

Macros can be run from within the VBA window, however, in this example we will create objects and assign the macro to the object and then run it from there.

Module 14

A rounded rectangle shape was added to the sheet and formatted with the second preset shape effect. Then with the shape selected, right click and select assign macro, then choose the correct macro. In this case, first. Select ok.

After the macro is assigned go back to the sheet and clear out what was added in c5, select a random cell, like d5 and click on the button.

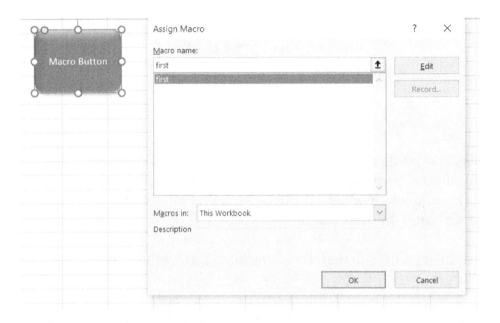

Delete the text and add two sheets to the workbook and create another macro, naming it second and record the following steps:

1. Enter A B C in cells A1, B1, C1 respectively
2. Select them all and click center and bold
3. In column A type 1, 2, 3 in rows 2 – 4
4. Copy all 3 values and paste to columns B and C
5. Select all of them, A1 to C4 and select Copy
6. Go to Sheet 2 and select cell A1 then click paste
7. Increase the column widths and row height
8. Change the color to Yellow
9. Return to Sheet 1, Cell A1
10. Stop Recording

Go into View Macro and View Macros and click Edit to view the code.

```
Sub second()
'
' second Macro
"   Range("A1").Select
    ActiveCell.FormulaR1C1 = "A"
    Range("B1").Select
    ActiveCell.FormulaR1C1 = "B"
    Range("C1").Select
    ActiveCell.FormulaR1C1 = "C"
    Range("A1:C1").Select
    Selection.Font.Bold = True
    With Selection
        .HorizontalAlignment = xlCenter
        .VerticalAlignment = xlBottom
        .WrapText = False
        .Orientation = 0
        .AddIndent = False
        .IndentLevel = 0
        .ShrinkToFit = False
        .ReadingOrder = xlContext
        .MergeCells = False
    End With
    Range("A2").Select
    ActiveCell.FormulaR1C1 = "1"
    Range("A3").Select
    ActiveCell.FormulaR1C1 = "2"
    Range("A4").Select
    ActiveCell.FormulaR1C1 = "3"
    Range("A2:A4").Select
    Selection.Copy
    Range("B2").Select
    ActiveSheet.Paste
    Range("C2").Select
    ActiveSheet.Paste
    Range("A1:C3").Select
    Application.CutCopyMode = False
    Range("A1:C4").Select
    Selection.Copy
    Sheets("Sheet2").Select
    ActiveSheet.Paste
    Columns("A:C").Select
    Selection.ColumnWidth = 12.78
    Rows("1:4").Select
    Selection.RowHeight = 27.6
    Range("A1:C4").Select
    Application.CutCopyMode = False
    With Selection.Interior
        .Pattern = xlSolid
        .PatternColorIndex = xlAutomatic
        .Color = 65535
        .TintAndShade = 0
        .PatternTintAndShade = 0
    End With
    Sheets("Sheet1").Select
    Range("A1").Select
End Sub
```

The Macro Code can be shown to the left. While it is much longer, knowing the steps we conducted, we can read through and get familiar with the methodology of the coding.

Specifically, paying attention to show sheets, cells and ranges are selected.

When it performs an operation within a cell that is currently selected, it starts with Active.Cell.

Module 14

Open the file Simple Macros to review some macros that can be used as they are or combined with other code.

The macro below deletes the contents of a selected cell. It combines with a message box so that the user doesn't accidentally clear a cell contents that is not desired.

```
Sub delete()
'

' delete Macro
'

Answer = MsgBox("This will delete cell
contents. Do you want to Continue?",
vbYesNoCancel + vbInformation, "Application
Message")
If Answer = vbYes Then Else Exit Sub


'

    Selection.ClearContents
End Sub
```

The macro below was created to demonstrate the macro on the next page that will replace a formula that is saved in another cell and format the cell to yellow fill in this case.

This macro is just deleting the contents which includes the formula and clears the yellow format.

```
Sub deleteclear()
'
' deleteclear Macro
'

'

    Range("E6").Select

    Selection.ClearContents

    With Selection.Interior
        .Pattern = xlSolid
        .PatternColorIndex = xlAutomatic
        .ThemeColor = xlThemeColorDark1
        .TintAndShade = 0
        .PatternTintAndShade = 0
    End With

    Range("E7").Select

End Sub
```

The macro below will replace a formula that is place in cell BE56 to cell E6. It also formats the cell fill as yellow. This concept is good to use to protect formulas from accidentally deleting in cases where cell protection is not used. Using cell BE was arbitrary but intended to demonstrate being in a spot that is far away from the main activity of the sheet.

```
Sub Replace2()
'
' Replace2 Macro
'


'

    Range("BE6").Select

    Selection.Copy



    Range("E6").Select

    ActiveSheet.Paste

    With Selection.Interior
        .Pattern = xlSolid
        .PatternColorIndex = xlAutomatic
        .Color = 65535
        .TintAndShade = 0
        .PatternTintAndShade = 0
    End With

    Range("E7").Select

End Sub
```

This code types value in a cell based on criteria.  The example is using Yes / No buttons.

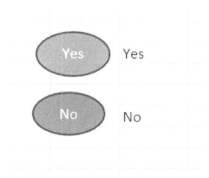

```
Sub Yes()
Range("K3").Select
    ActiveCell.FormulaR1C1 = "Yes"
    Range("L3").Select
End Sub


Sub No()
Range("K6").Select
    ActiveCell.FormulaR1C1 = "No"
    Range("L6").Select
End Sub
```

The code below goes on the worksheet instead of the module. What it performs is that when a cell value is selected, it populates the designated cell with the value indicated. For example, when M2 is selected, a 1 is put in N2.

The main part of this code, highlighted below, can be copied and pasted to create other cells with the functionality. Only the cell references have to be changed. This can be practice in the gray highlighted cells.

```
Private Sub Worksheet_SelectionChange(ByVal Target
As Range)

If Target.Address = "$M$2" Then
Range("N2") = "1"
End If

If Target.Address = "$M$3" Then
Range("N3") = "2"
End If

If Target.Address = "$M$4" Then
Range("N4") = "3"
End If
End Sub
```

|  | Resulting Cell |
|---|---|
| Target Address 1 |  |
| Target Address 2 |  |
| Target Address 3 |  |
| Target Address 4 |  |
| Target Address 5 |  |

The message box code below can be used separately or in combination with other macros like shown in the prior examples.

```
Sub MessageBox()

Answer = MsgBox("Hello this is a message box! Click to
continue.", vbYesNoCancel + vbInformation,
"Application Message")
If Answer = vbYes Then Else Exit Sub

End Sub
```

Macros do not always run and troubleshooting and debugging is required.

The example below shows and error message. The code will also be highlighted in yellow. To clear the debugger, the little square needs to be clicked. (it is circled in pink)

The code can also be run from inside the VBA by clicking the arrow or run.

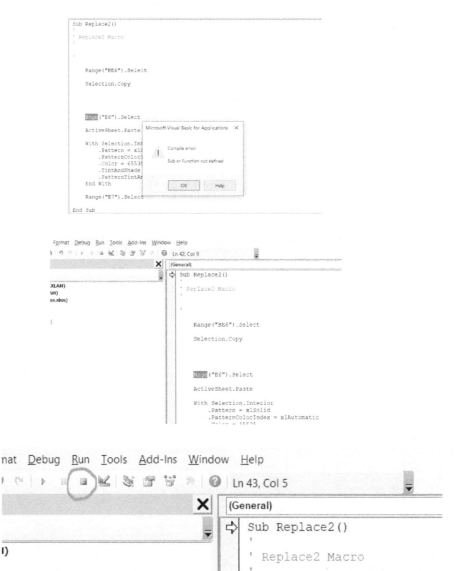

# Summary: Module 14

Macros are programs created in Microsoft Excel's Visual Basic Application (VBA) language. Getting start with macros can be accomplished by recording some specific steps and assigning it to a shape, image or object or by copying existing code.

Various codes can be combined to create additional functionality. Often an internet search can produce pieces of code that can be modified and placed into a current spreadsheet.

It is recommended to review the code and the written steps in order to get familiar with the format and conventions used in the VBA language. Often times a code can be expanded by copying and pasting sections and then adding modifications.

Sometimes macros are place within modules and others they go into an area for that specific sheet's code.

The Visual Basic code can be viewed in a project explorer which can be accessed by right clicking on a sheet and selecting "view code" as well as the View Macro menu steps.

Debugging errors is a common part of the process and error message along with highlights can assist with the troubleshooting. Sometimes an internet search of the error message can help diagnose and resolve the issues.

Macro security is important, and macros should only be run from trusted sources.

The file that contains macros needs to be saved as a macro enabled workbook which is available in the save as option within the File Menu.

# Module 15

- Working with Data Sets – Loading Transactions

# Case Study: Loader Daily Report

# Process Improvement

The following use case, is inspired from a distribution project where each person with the job of loading and shipping the items has a goal related to how many cases they are able to process in one hour,  In this example, they are called Loaders and Shippers,  Each individual is assigned a UsserId and each transaction they perform on loading or shipping is tracked in the Warehouse Management System (WMS).  The product in the example case is colored beads.

In order to monitor production on a team and individual level a daily report was generated and sent out by email.  The individual that created the report would run a report on their computer from the WMS and manually count the transactions per person.  The process took 40 minutes to 1 hour daily.

The other opportunity with the manual tracking, was that no history of the data was able to be reviewed to identify opportunities or improvements either on an individual or team level.

Below shows a modified subset of a report that is available for download directly from the system.

This example will show how using Microsoft Excel techniques and functionality, the process was reduced to less than 5 minutes and much more  valuable process information was obtained and able to be utilized.

| Record ID | Item | Quantity | Transaction Start | Transaction End | LoginID |
|---|---|---|---|---|---|
| 78 | Red | 2 | 2023-07-11 06:42:27 | 2023-07-11 06:44:16 | PERSON3 |
| 79 | Blue | 1 | 2023-07-11 06:44:16 | 2023-07-11 06:45:10 | PERSON3 |
| 80 | Blue | 3 | 2023-07-11 06:49:40 | 2023-07-11 06:50:31 | PERSON3 |
| 81 | Blue | 1 | 2023-07-11 06:50:32 | 2023-07-11 06:55:28 | PERSON3 |
| 82 | Yellow | 3 | 2023-07-11 07:01:04 | 2023-07-11 07:01:51 | PERSON3 |
| 83 | Yellow | 2 | 2023-07-11 07:01:52 | 2023-07-11 07:03:40 | PERSON3 |
| 84 | Yellow | 1 | 2023-07-11 07:07:31 | 2023-07-11 07:08:08 | PERSON3 |
| 85 | Red | 3 | 2023-07-11 07:10:09 | 2023-07-11 07:11:24 | PERSON3 |
| 86 | Blue | 2 | 2023-07-11 07:11:25 | 2023-07-11 07:14:33 | PERSON3 |
| 87 | Green | 15 | 2023-07-11 07:17:01 | 2023-07-11 07:18:25 | PERSON3 |
| 88 | Yellow | 60 | 2023-07-11 07:18:26 | 2023-07-11 07:19:49 | PERSON3 |
| 89 | Red | 1 | 2023-07-11 07:22:34 | 2023-07-11 07:23:05 | PERSON3 |
| 90 | Red | 10 | 2023-07-11 07:28:10 | 2023-07-11 07:28:50 | PERSON3 |
| 91 | Red | 24 | 2023-07-11 07:50:04 | 2023-07-11 07:51:13 | PERSON3 |
| 92 | Red | 1 | 2023-07-11 07:52:51 | 2023-07-11 07:53:27 | PERSON3 |
| 93 | Blue | 2 | 2023-07-11 07:53:27 | 2023-07-11 07:56:09 | PERSON3 |
| 94 | Blue | 1 | 2023-07-11 08:04:04 | 2023-07-11 08:04:51 | PERSON3 |
| 95 | Blue | 3 | 2023-07-11 08:20:15 | 2023-07-11 08:20:49 | PERSON3 |
| 96 | Yellow | 5 | 2023-07-11 08:20:50 | 2023-07-11 08:23:34 | PERSON3 |

# Understanding the Data

The first step when working to streamline a data acquisition and reporting process is to understand the structure of the data and how the resulting numbers are obtained.

Each transaction represents a case processed by the different user and this is what goals and targets are based upon.

Usually, system generated information contains many fields of information that may not be needed; however, it is ok to take the data the way it is an just use the columns and fields required. The download was modified and simplified for example purposes.

The highlighted example below shows approximately 1 hour of transactions by userid, Person3. The first transaction started at 6:04 and by 7:51 had processed 14 cases. Simplified for example purposes, this is approximately 14 cases / hour.

The solution was set up based on this type of data.

While there are often many ways to accomplish an objective, the methods demonstrated in this highlight some key functionality that is very effective. As we step through the example, focus on the formulas and processes used to get the end result while keeping in mind this is just one way to accomplish an improved process.

| Record ID | Item | Quantity | Transaction Start | Transaction End | LoginID | | |
|---|---|---|---|---|---|---|---|
| 78 | Red | 2 | 2023-07-11 06:42:27 | 2023-07-11 06:44:16 | PERSON3 | | 6:42 AM |
| 79 | Blue | 1 | 2023-07-11 06:44:16 | 2023-07-11 06:45:10 | PERSON3 | | |
| 80 | Blue | 3 | 2023-07-11 06:49:40 | 2023-07-11 06:50:31 | PERSON3 | | |
| 81 | Blue | 1 | 2023-07-11 06:50:32 | 2023-07-11 06:55:28 | PERSON3 | | |
| 82 | Yellow | 3 | 2023-07-11 07:01:04 | 2023-07-11 07:01:51 | PERSON3 | | |
| 83 | Yellow | 2 | 2023-07-11 07:01:52 | 2023-07-11 07:03:40 | PERSON3 | | |
| 84 | Yellow | 1 | 2023-07-11 07:07:31 | 2023-07-11 07:08:08 | PERSON3 | | |
| 85 | Red | 3 | 2023-07-11 07:10:09 | 2023-07-11 07:11:24 | PERSON3 | | |
| 86 | Blue | 2 | 2023-07-11 07:11:25 | 2023-07-11 07:14:33 | PERSON3 | | |
| 87 | Green | 15 | 2023-07-11 07:17:01 | 2023-07-11 07:18:25 | PERSON3 | | |
| 88 | Yellow | 60 | 2023-07-11 07:18:26 | 2023-07-11 07:19:49 | PERSON3 | | |
| 89 | Red | 1 | 2023-07-11 07:22:34 | 2023-07-11 07:23:05 | PERSON3 | | |
| 90 | Red | 10 | 2023-07-11 07:28:10 | 2023-07-11 07:28:50 | PERSON3 | | |
| 91 | Red | 24 | 2023-07-11 07:50:04 | 2023-07-11 07:51:13 | PERSON3 | 14 | 7:51 AM |

# Strategizing an Approach

The user readily has access to the system and can download the reports. The decision was made to use Power Query and have the daily reports saved and pulled into an Excel Spreadsheet.

When creating a connection to a folder using Power Query, the resulting table has the source name which is the name of the file in the first column. This example will demonstrate how utilizing a consistent naming convention can allow for the field to be used and provide valuable information, as well.

We will start by setting up the data connection, pull. A folder was set up named ReportPull and a 4 days worth of reports were put inside to use to build the spreadsheet.

## ReportPull

Name

- 071023
- 071123
- 071223
- 071323

The naming convention for the daily file used is MMDDYY and this consistent naming will be able to be used within the spreadsheet.

Next the query will be set up.

# Setting Up the Folder and Files

The file is saved in a folder that is dedicated to the folders and files related to this use case. It is being saved as a Macro-Enabled File as Visual Basic Macros will be used to facilitate the process and help make it more efficient.

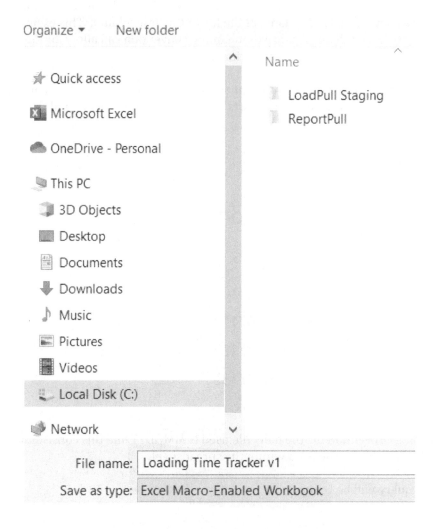

# Setting Up the Query

To set up the query, File > Get Data > From File > From Folder

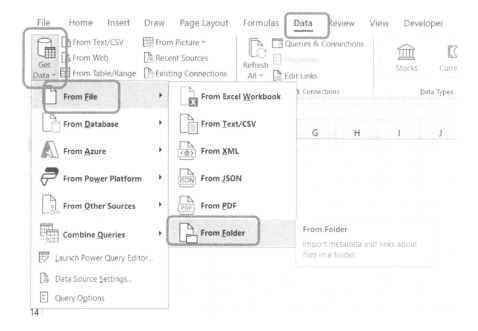

Navigate to the Folder and Select the correct one and click Open

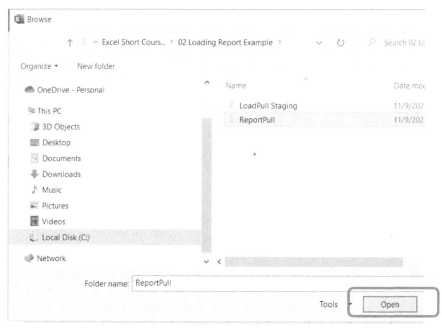

## Review the files in the folder and select "Combine and Load"

## Select the correct sheet, review the preview and click Ok

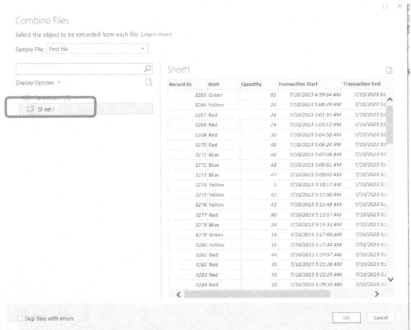

# Review Query Pull Results

## Data

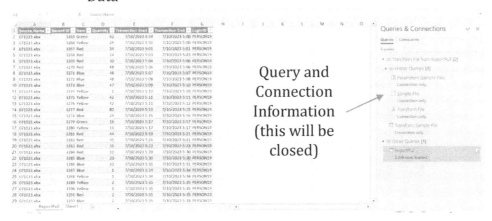

Query and
Connection
Information
(this will be
closed)

## Set up Table and Write the Formulas

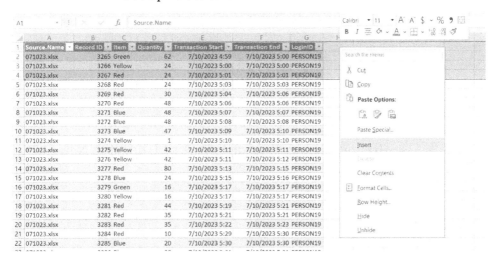

Insert 4 Rows at the top – select the entire row (1 – 4) and Right Click > Insert
This practice allows space for organization purposes.

## Setting Up Formulas

Since we are counting the number of transactions per person in order, to make the logic work, sorting is required.

| Source.Name | Record ID | Item | Quantity | Transaction Start | Transaction End | LoginID |
|---|---|---|---|---|---|---|
| 071123.xlsx | 21336 | Yellow | 4 | 7/11/2023 7:46 | 7/11/2023 7:50 | PERSON1 |
| 071123.xlsx | 21337 | Red | 1 | 7/11/2023 7:50 | 7/11/2023 7:52 | PERSON1 |
| 071123.xlsx | 21338 | Blue | 2 | 7/11/2023 7:52 | 7/11/2023 7:53 | PERSON1 |
| 071123.xlsx | 21339 | Green | 1 | 7/11/2023 7:55 | 7/11/2023 7:58 | PERSON1 |
| 071123.xlsx | 21340 | Yellow | 4 | 7/11/2023 7:59 | 7/11/2023 8:01 | PERSON1 |
| 071123.xlsx | 21341 | Red | 46 | 7/11/2023 8:03 | 7/11/2023 8:05 | PERSON1 |
| 071123.xlsx | 21342 | Red | 6 | 7/11/2023 8:06 | 7/11/2023 8:07 | PERSON1 |
| 071123.xlsx | 21343 | Red | 2 | 7/11/2023 8:08 | 7/11/2023 8:12 | PERSON1 |
| 071123.xlsx | 21344 | Red | 4 | 7/11/2023 8:53 | 7/11/2023 9:39 | PERSON1 |
| 071123.xlsx | 21345 | Blue | 1 | 7/11/2023 9:47 | 7/11/2023 9:47 | PERSON1 |
| 071123.xlsx | 21346 | Blue | 5 | 7/11/2023 9:47 | 7/11/2023 9:48 | PERSON1 |
| 071123.xlsx | 21347 | Blue | 10 | 7/11/2023 9:48 | 7/11/2023 9:50 | PERSON1 |
| 071123.xlsx | 21348 | Yellow | 2 | 7/11/2023 9:50 | 7/11/2023 9:51 | PERSON1 |
| 071123.xlsx | 21349 | Yellow | 1 | 7/11/2023 9:51 | 7/11/2023 9:52 | PERSON1 |
| 071123.xlsx | 21350 | Yellow | 1 | 7/11/2023 9:52 | 7/11/2023 9:52 | PERSON1 |
| 071123.xlsx | 21351 | Red | 1 | 7/11/2023 9:52 | 7/11/2023 9:53 | PERSON1 |
| 071123.xlsx | 21352 | Blue | 60 | 7/11/2023 10:54 | 7/11/2023 10:59 | PERSON1 |
| 071123.xlsx | 21353 | Green | 10 | 7/11/2023 10:59 | 7/11/2023 11:00 | PERSON1 |
| 071123.xlsx | 21354 | Yellow | 58 | 7/11/2023 11:00 | 7/11/2023 11:15 | PERSON1 |

## Multi-level Sort
Data > Sort
Click on the Window

Sort

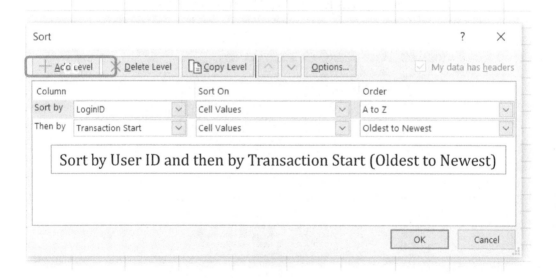

Concatenate (Join)
A join formula will be used to make a combination of User and Transaction Date. Prior to that we will set up the date formulas.

This table will be maintained as a dynamic table and the formulas will reference the column name vs cell reference. Upon selecting the cell when writing the formula, Excel formats the reference correctly. The step is the same as if the cell address was being referenced. It just takes some getting used to!

Below shows the formulas. The components of a Date Year, Month, Week and Day were pulled off of the Transaction Start Date / Time. Then to just have a stand-alone Date, not Date / Time the Date formula was used. See formulas below.

| Year | | Month | | Week | |
|---|---|---|---|---|---|
| =YEAR([@[Transaction Start]]) | | =MONTH([@[Transaction Start]]) | | =WEEKNUM([@[Transaction Start]]) | |

| Day | | Date | | Join | |
|---|---|---|---|---|---|
| =DAY([@[Transaction Start]]) | | =DATE([@Year],[@Month],[@Day]) | | =[@LoginID]&[@Date] | |

As a quick reminder, to show these formulas within the cell a single quote ' was placed in front of them. After screen shots were made, the single quote was removed.

'=YEAR([@[Transaction Start]])

A formula is written, called Sequence, that looks to see if the transaction start / user combination is of the same user and date. If it is then it increments by 1 if not it goes to 1.

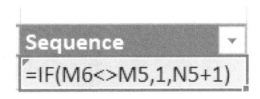

**Sequence**
=IF(M6<>M5,1,N5+1)

The result of the Sequence formula can be seen below.

| | LoginID | Year | Month | Week | Day | Date | Join | Sequence | |
|---|---|---|---|---|---|---|---|---|---|
| 15 | PERSON14 | 2023 | 7 | 28 | 10 | 7/10/2023 | PERSON1445117 | 140 | |
| 16 | PERSON14 | 2023 | 7 | 28 | 10 | 7/10/2023 | PERSON1445117 | 141 | |
| 21 | PERSON14 | 2023 | 7 | 28 | 10 | 7/10/2023 | PERSON1445117 | 142 | |
| 22 | PERSON14 | 2023 | 7 | 28 | 10 | 7/10/2023 | PERSON1445117 | 143 | |
| 25 | PERSON14 | 2023 | 7 | 28 | 10 | 7/10/2023 | PERSON1445117 | 144 | |
| 47 | PERSON14 | 2023 | 7 | 28 | 10 | 7/10/2023 | PERSON1445117 | 145 | |
| 15 | PERSON15 | 2023 | 7 | 28 | 10 | 7/10/2023 | PERSON1545117 | 1 | |
| 16 | PERSON15 | 2023 | 7 | 28 | 10 | 7/10/2023 | PERSON1545117 | 2 | |
| 17 | PERSON15 | 2023 | 7 | 28 | 10 | 7/10/2023 | PERSON1545117 | 3 | |

It is important to note that the success and accuracy of this formula depends on the data being sorted correctly by User and Date. A safety mechanism should be considered and added prior to completing the solution.

It can be noted that the lowest number of the sequence, which will be 1, in each case is the first transaction for that person on a given day. The last number, in this example for Person 14 is 145 which is the highest (maximum) number of the sequence will indicate the total number of transactions (cases) that were processed.

The MIN and MAX formulas on sequence will be used in conjunction with a pivot table to calculate the number of cases processed per person on a given day.

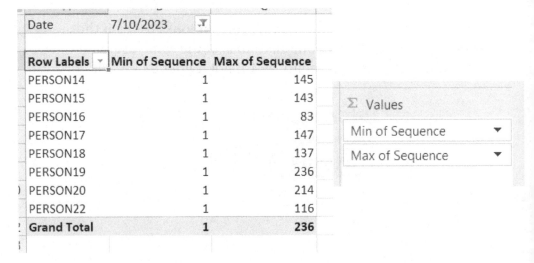

| Date | 7/10/2023 | |
|---|---|---|
| **Row Labels** | **Min of Sequence** | **Max of Sequence** |
| PERSON14 | 1 | 145 |
| PERSON15 | 1 | 143 |
| PERSON16 | 1 | 83 |
| PERSON17 | 1 | 147 |
| PERSON18 | 1 | 137 |
| PERSON19 | 1 | 236 |
| PERSON20 | 1 | 214 |
| PERSON22 | 1 | 116 |
| **Grand Total** | **1** | **236** |

Σ Values

Min of Sequence ▼

Max of Sequence ▼

Changing the Pivot Table Field Value Settings can be performed using different methods.

The drop-down arrow next to the value field settings can be opened and the mathematical operation can be changed. In this case the sequence is changed to Min and then another instance of Sequence is added, and that value field setting is changed to Max.

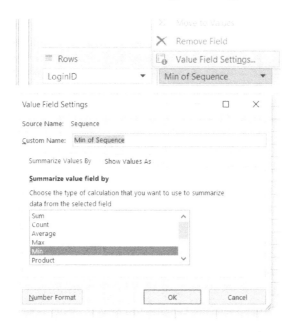

A short cut tot the value field settings can be performed by "Double Clicking" on the Column Header. In this case Double Clicking on Max of Sequence header will open up the dialogue box.

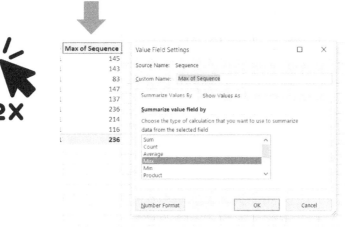

Validating the Results in the Table

| Date | 7/10/2023 | |
| --- | --- | --- |
| | | |
| Row Labels | Min of Sequence | Max of Sequence |
| PERSON14 | 1 | 145 |
| PERSON15 | 1 | 143 |
| PERSON16 | 1 | 83 |
| PERSON17 | 1 | 147 |
| PERSON18 | 1 | 137 |
| PERSON19 | 1 | 236 |
| PERSON20 | 1 | 214 |
| PERSON22 | 1 | 116 |
| Grand Total | 1 | 236 |

This table is validated by adding a report filter to the pivot table for Date and then going back to the raw data download and adding a filter. Set the filter to Date 7/1/23 and Person 14.

Freeze Panes was also utilized so the filter would also be visible when scrolling.  It can be seen that the numbers match at 145 for Person 14 on date 7/10/23

| Source.Name | Record ID | Item | Quantity | Transaction Start | Transaction End | LoginID | Year | Month | Week | Day | Date | Join | Sequence |
| --- | --- | --- | --- | --- | --- | --- | --- | --- | --- | --- | --- | --- | --- |
| 071023.xlsx | 13879 | Red | 19 | 7/10/2023 14:05 | 7/10/2023 14:08 | PERSON14 | 2023 | 7 | 28 | 10 | 7/10/2023 | PERSON1445117 | 136 |
| 071023.xlsx | 13880 | Red | 16 | 7/10/2023 14:09 | 7/10/2023 14:10 | PERSON14 | 2023 | 7 | 28 | 10 | 7/10/2023 | PERSON1445117 | 137 |
| 071023.xlsx | 13881 | Red | 7 | 7/10/2023 14:11 | 7/10/2023 14:11 | PERSON14 | 2023 | 7 | 28 | 10 | 7/10/2023 | PERSON1445117 | 138 |
| 071023.xlsx | 13882 | Red | 7 | 7/10/2023 14:11 | 7/10/2023 14:11 | PERSON14 | 2023 | 7 | 28 | 10 | 7/10/2023 | PERSON1445117 | 139 |
| 071023.xlsx | 13883 | Blue | 12 | 7/10/2023 14:13 | 7/10/2023 14:15 | PERSON14 | 2023 | 7 | 28 | 10 | 7/10/2023 | PERSON1445117 | 140 |
| 071023.xlsx | 13884 | Blue | 45 | 7/10/2023 14:15 | 7/10/2023 14:16 | PERSON14 | 2023 | 7 | 28 | 10 | 7/10/2023 | PERSON1445117 | 141 |
| 071023.xlsx | 13885 | Blue | 10 | 7/10/2023 14:20 | 7/10/2023 14:21 | PERSON14 | 2023 | 7 | 28 | 10 | 7/10/2023 | PERSON1445117 | 142 |
| 071023.xlsx | 13886 | Yellow | 50 | 7/10/2023 14:22 | 7/10/2023 14:22 | PERSON14 | 2023 | 7 | 28 | 10 | 7/10/2023 | PERSON1445117 | 143 |
| 071023.xlsx | 13887 | Yellow | 10 | 7/10/2023 14:24 | 7/10/2023 14:25 | PERSON14 | 2023 | 7 | 28 | 10 | 7/10/2023 | PERSON1445117 | 144 |
| 071023.xlsx | 13888 | Yellow | 73 | 7/10/2023 14:45 | 7/10/2023 14:47 | PERSON14 | 2023 | 7 | 28 | 10 | 7/10/2023 | PERSON1445117 | 145 |
| 071023.xlsx | 24143 | Red | 18 | 7/10/2023 6:13 | 7/10/2023 6:15 | PERSON15 | 2023 | 7 | 28 | 10 | 7/10/2023 | PERSON1545117 | 1 |

VLOOKUP for name instead of userid

| Date | 7/10/2023 | |
|---|---|---|
| | | |
| Row Labels | Min of Sequence | Max of Sequence |
| PERSON14 | 1 | 145 |
| PERSON15 | 1 | 143 |
| PERSON16 | 1 | 83 |
| PERSON17 | 1 | 147 |
| PERSON18 | 1 | 137 |
| PERSON19 | 1 | 236 |
| PERSON20 | 1 | 214 |
| PERSON22 | 1 | 116 |
| Grand Total | 1 | 236 |

Upon review of the table, it is noted that having the person's name would be more valuable than the Userid, therefore a VLOOKUP and a table will be created to pull in the person's name.

A sheet was added called Users, and will house a cross reference between the userid and the person's name. It is colored black as a workbook organization technique. Indicating that reference sheets with information or for lookup tables are black. The color is arbitrary but that is what is used in this example.

User Id – Person's Name Reference Table
See table below.  An additional field reference the individual's role was also included.

| UserID | Name | Role |
|---|---|---|
| PERSON1 | Tristin Castillo | Loader |
| PERSON2 | Kamari Hayden | Loader |
| PERSON3 | Maddox Terry | Loader |
| PERSON4 | Carmen Swanson | Loader |
| PERSON5 | Rhys Bates | Loader |
| PERSON6 | Miles Duncan | Loader |
| PERSON7 | Shawn Mcconnell | Loader |
| PERSON8 | Jazmyn Winters | Loader |
| PERSON9 | Larissa Barber | Loader |
| PERSON10 | Sabrina Jenkins | Loader |
| PERSON11 | Camille Weaver | Loader |
| PERSON12 | Billy Ellis | Loader |
| PERSON13 | Juliana Mccann | Loader |
| PERSON14 | Kaylyn Leach | Packer |
| PERSON15 | Eden Meadows | Packer |
| PERSON16 | Nigel Mayer | Packer |
| PERSON17 | Ellis Caldwell | Packer |
| PERSON18 | Meadow Donovan | Packer |
| PERSON19 | Laney Floyd | Packer |

A VLOOKUP to the main sheet can now be created.

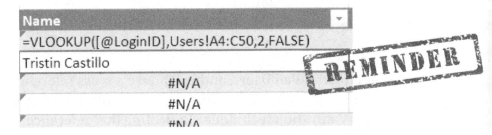

Reminder: Looking at this formula for the vlookup, there are no $ in the table reference A4 to C50.  This is because the sheet containing the table is part of the same workbook as the sheet we are pulling it into and Excel doesn't automatically put the $.  The $ signs are to make the table and absolute reference and always chose the same range regardless of where the formula is copied to. I can be noted that at the 3rd record, an #NA was returned.

VLOOKUP – continued
It can be seen that in the cell with the first #NA the table
reference is starting at 6 and person 1 is on row 5 in the lookup
table. Because there were no $ or absolute reference, the
formula values shifted as the formula was copied to lower rows.

Manually adding the $ will correct that.

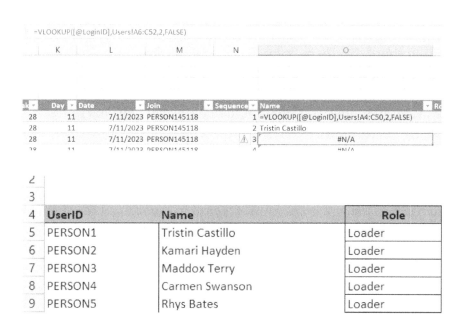

Another practice that can be utilized is extending the lookup
table reference beyond the actual table. This allows for any
additions to be included without having to change formulas.

It can be noted that the formula was taken to row 50 extended
beyond row 31 of the current table.

=IFERROR(VLOOKUP([@LoginID],Users!$A$4:$C$50,2,FALSE),"")

IFERROR: Another practice commonly used is the IFERROR formula in front of formulas. This will prevent any error values to show up as #NA. An easy way to apply the formula is after you have completed the formula and tested if it works correctly, go to the beginning right after the = sign and type Iferro( then go to the end of the formula and type , "") This will put a blank value instead of an error. Other things can be put in there. Some people use messages like check or review and others put values so then can flag errors.

The blank is good to use as it will not affect any calculations if there is math being performed on that column.

Adding the Vlookup formula for the role.
Since the formula to pull in the role based on the userid is very similar to the one for name the 'quote technique was used to move the formula to that cell.

Once moved the single quote is removed and the return value is changed from 2 to 3 in this case. Initiating that the formula returns the value from the 3rd column in the table when it finds a match on userid.

| | Name | Role | |
|---|---|---|---|
| 1 | Tristin Castillo | =IFERROR VLOOKUP([@LoginID],Users!$A$4:$C$50,2,FALSE),"") | |
| 2 | Tristin Castillo | | |

Rate per Hour Formula

Since it is desired, that we have a metric of cases per hour. It is required that the total time be calculated. The functionality of looking at the time between transactions, as well as transaction time will be calculated.

In addition to the single quote ' method to turn a formula into text for review of the details. There is show formula feature within Excel that will highlight every formula on the sheet.

This technique was used to show all of the formulas written to extract the time components in order to build a stand alone time field. The formulas can be seen below. To return back, just click the show formulas icon again.

To create the time, each component of time was extracted from the date time cell and then put back together using the TIME() formula.

The IFERROR can also be placed around each of these as a precaution.

Using the first formula to create the second on for the time between transaction minutes.

The dynamic tables are very powerful. The formula in AG was copied using the single quote ' and then modified using the dynamic table reference. Once the TT was started to be changed, Excel brought up potential fields. Then you just click on the correct one to enter into the formula. This is great to use when there are many similar formulas that need to be modified.

=([@[BT Hour]]*60)+[@[bT Min]]+([@[TT Sec]]/60)

| AB | AC | AD | AF | AG | AH | AI |
|---|---|---|---|---|---|---|
| | | (...) BT Hour | | | | |
| | | (...) BT Min | | | | |
| | | (...) BT Sec | | | | |

| T Min | TT Sec | BT Hou | BT Min | BT Sec | Minutes of Transaction | Minutes Between Transactio |
|---|---|---|---|---|---|---|
| .002465 | 1.000003 | | | 0 | | 0.02 | 60)+[@[bT |
| .001354 | 1.000001 | 0 | 0 | 0 | 0.02 | |
| .000625 | 1 | 0 | 1.16E-05 | 1 | 0.02 | |
| .002072 | 1.000002 | 0 | 0.001586 | 17 | 0.02 | |

Now that the main formulas have been added, the Pivot Table will be set up to create the Daily Summary report. Usually after fields are added when the pivot table is already set up. The table needs to be "Refreshed" so that the fields will show up in the list.

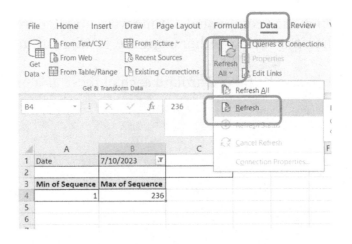

The Grand Total was removed by "Right Click" on the grand total row and selecting Remove Grand Total.

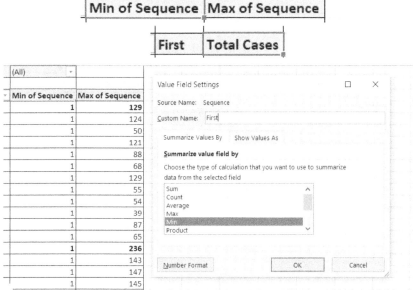

The titles for these can be changed by double clicking on them and adding a custom name. If you ever need to find out what the original name was, just double check and it will be in source name.

| Min of Sequence | Max of Sequence |
|---|---|

| First | Total Cases |
|---|---|

The main summary table in this example will be a combination of a pivot table and some formulas outside that use pivot table information. The daily summary report will be created.

The table is filter using the report filter on a single date. The daily summary is designed to only be a single date but having the data available for all allows for filtering to different days and for other trending that will be on separate sheets.

A sumifs formula is being used below to pull in the time for the first and last case transaction. Since there is only one first and one last the summing operation will work. The sequence number for the first and last case is used as the criteria in combination with the person's name.

A formula was added to the front of the sumifs to create a blank cell if it is the header of Packer or Loader.

| Date | 7/10/2023 ⊽ | | | |
|---|---|---|---|---|
| | | | | |
| Row Labels ▾ | First | Total Cases | Time First Case | Time Last Case |
| ⊟ Packer | 1 | 236 | | |
| Eden Meadows | 1 | 143 | 6:13:28 AM | 2:14:43 PM |
| Ellis Caldwell | 1 | 147 | 5:11:16 AM | 3:13:16 PM |
| Kaylyn Leach | 1 | 145 | 4:56:25 AM | 2:47:22 PM |
| Laney Floyd | 1 | 236 | 4:59:24 AM | 2:53:29 PM |
| Maverick Dixon | 1 | 214 | 5:11:46 AM | 2:52:05 PM |
| Meadow Donovan | 1 | 137 | 5:11:42 AM | 1:17:28 PM |
| Nigel Mayer | 1 | 83 | 6:19:42 AM | 2:17:52 PM |
| Steve Anderson | 1 | 116 | 6:19:21 AM | 2:18:47 PM |

The sumifs formula sums the main range of start time is shown below:

> =IF(OR(A5="Packer",A5="Loader"),"",SUMIFS(ReportPull[[#All],[Start Time]],ReportPull[[#All],[Sequence]],'Daily Summary'!B5,ReportPull[[#All],[Date]],'Daily Summary'!$B$1,ReportPull[[#All],[Name]],'Daily Summary'!A5))

The sumifs formula sums the main range of end time is shown below:

> =IF(OR(A5="Packer",A5="Loader"),"",SUMIFS(ReportPull[[#All],[End Time]],ReportPull[[#All],[Sequence]],'Daily Summary'!C5,ReportPull[[#All],[Date]],'Daily Summary'!$B$1,ReportPull[[#All],[Name]],'Daily Summary'!A5))

The structure of these formulas is very similar. The only difference is the use of start vs stop time and the first or last sequence number.

The next calculation added to the table is the actual working time which is the time from the start of the first transaction to the end of the last transaction. Two different methods are being shown in order to practice working with time and calculations with time. For the actual use case duplicate calculations will not be necessary and columns will be hidden for this example.

| Date | 7/10/2023 | | | | | | | | | |
|---|---|---|---|---|---|---|---|---|---|---|
| Row Labels | First | Total Cases | Time First Case | Time Last Case | Calc | Hour | Min | Sec | Worked Time | Work Time Calc 24 |
| Packer | 1 | 236 | | | | | | | | |
| Eden Meadows | 1 | 143 | 6:13:28 AM | 2:14:43 PM | 8:01:15 | 8 | 1 | 15 | 8.02 | 8.02 |
| Ellis Caldwell | 1 | 147 | 5:11:16 AM | 3:13:16 PM | 10:02:00 | 10 | 2 | 0 | 10.03 | 10.03 |
| Kaylyn Leach | 1 | 145 | 4:56:25 AM | 2:47:22 PM | 9:50:57 | 9 | 50 | 57 | 9.85 | 9.85 |
| Laney Floyd | 1 | 236 | 4:59:24 AM | 2:53:29 PM | 9:54:05 | 9 | 54 | 5 | 9.90 | 9.90 |
| Maverick Dixon | 1 | 214 | 5:11:46 AM | 2:52:05 PM | 9:40:19 | 9 | 40 | 19 | 9.67 | 9.67 |
| Meadow Donovan | 1 | 137 | 5:11:42 AM | 1:17:28 PM | 8:05:46 | 8 | 5 | 46 | 8.10 | 8.10 |
| Nigel Mayer | 1 | 83 | 6:19:42 AM | 2:17:52 PM | 7:58:10 | 7 | 58 | 10 | 7.97 | 7.97 |
| Steve Anderson | 1 | 116 | 6:19:21 AM | 2:18:47 PM | 7:59:26 | 7 | 59 | 26 | 7.99 | 7.99 |

The formula in F5 is taking the difference between the Last and First transaction time. It is formatted using the time format shown below. This type of format is suitable for viewing the result as in this case as we can see 8 hours and 1 minute. However, it can present some challenges when trying to graph and trend so converting it to an hour number with decimals will be shown. It can be any units, but it this example hour will be used.

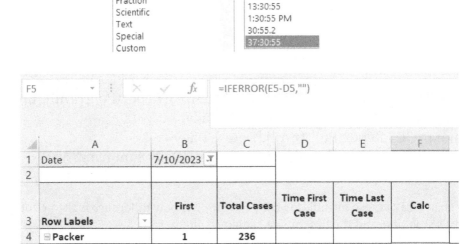

| F5 | ▾ | ⋮ | ✕ | ✓ | $f_x$ | =IFERROR(E5-D5,"") |

|  | A | B | C | D | E | F |
|---|---|---|---|---|---|---|
| 1 | Date | 7/10/2023 ⊤ |  |  |  |  |
| 2 |  |  |  |  |  |  |
| 3 | Row Labels ▾ | First | Total Cases | Time First Case | Time Last Case | Calc |
| 4 | ⊟Packer | 1 | 236 |  |  |  |
| 5 | Eden Meadows | 1 | 143 | 6:13:28 AM | 2:14:43 PM | 8:01:15 |
| 6 | Ellis Caldwell | 1 | 147 | 5:11:16 AM | 3:13:16 PM | 10:02:00 |
| 7 | Kaylyn Leach | 1 | 145 | 4:56:25 AM | 2:47:22 PM | 9:50:57 |
| 8 | Laney Floyd | 1 | 236 | 4:59:24 AM | 2:53:29 PM | 9:54:05 |
| 9 | Maverick Dixon | 1 | 214 | 5:11:46 AM | 2:52:05 PM | 9:40:19 |
| 10 | Meadow Donovan | 1 | 137 | 5:11:42 AM | 1:17:28 PM | 8:05:46 |
| 11 | Nigel Mayer | 1 | 83 | 6:19:42 AM | 2:17:52 PM | 7:58:10 |
| 12 | Steve Anderson | 1 | 116 | 6:19:21 AM | 2:18:47 PM | 7:59:26 |
| 13 |  |  |  |  |  |  |

The formulas to extract the components of time are used in subsequent columns.  = HOUR, =MINUTE, and = SECOND were utilized. They all follow the same format and have the formula in the front that looks for a blank value and returns and blank if that is true.

$$=IF(F5="","",HOUR(F5))$$

| Calc | Hour | Min | Sec |
|---|---|---|---|
| 8:01:15 | 8 | 1 | 15 |
| 10:02:00 | 10 | 2 | 0 |

The hours were then calculated using each component of time. The hours plus the minutes divided by 60 and the seconds divided by 3600. This is a great practice with use of parenthesis in Excel. The iferror statement was added on to the beginning to return a blank if the formula cannot calculate due to blank cells.

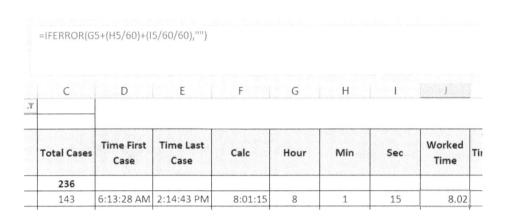

=IFERROR(G5+(H5/60)+(I5/60/60),"")

| | C | D | E | F | G | H | I | J |
|---|---|---|---|---|---|---|---|---|
| | Total Cases | Time First Case | Time Last Case | Calc | Hour | Min | Sec | Worked Time | Tir |
| | 236 | | | | | | | | |
| | 143 | 6:13:28 AM | 2:14:43 PM | 8:01:15 | 8 | 1 | 15 | 8.02 | |

Since Excel numbers are registered as serial numbers with midnight being 0, the difference of the two times multiplied by 24 will give that time difference in decimal hours. The formula in pink below demonstrates this. It can be seen that both calculations match.

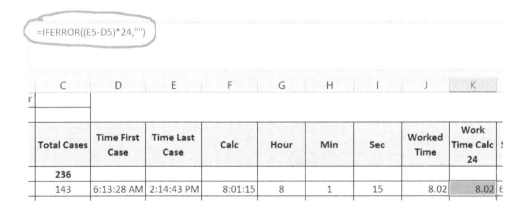

=IFERROR((E5-D5)*24,"")

| | C | D | E | F | G | H | I | J | K |
|---|---|---|---|---|---|---|---|---|---|
| | Total Cases | Time First Case | Time Last Case | Calc | Hour | Min | Sec | Worked Time | Work Time Calc 24 |
| | 236 | | | | | | | | |
| | 143 | 6:13:28 AM | 2:14:43 PM | 8:01:15 | 8 | 1 | 15 | 8.02 | 8.02 |

Replicating formulas two different ways was only conducted for example purposes. Normally, duplicate calculates would not be part of the solution.

The calculation of actual work time has been calculated and now we will look at the total time the person was clocked in and being paid for hours. Fields were added to the lookup table by person to indicate their respective shift start and end times.

This was pulled into the table using a VLOOKUP.

| UserID | Name | Role | Start Time | End Time |
|---|---|---|---|---|
| PERSON1 | Tristin Castillo | Loader | 4:00 AM | 12:30 PM |
| PERSON2 | Kamari Hayden | Loader | 5:00 AM | 1:30 PM |
| PERSON3 | Maddox Terry | Loader | 6:00 AM | 2:30 PM |
| PERSON4 | Carmen Swanson | Loader | 6:00 AM | 2:30 PM |
| PERSON5 | Rhys Bates | Loader | 6:00 AM | 2:30 PM |
| PERSON6 | Miles Duncan | Loader | 6:00 AM | 2:30 PM |
| PERSON7 | Shawn Mcconnell | Loader | 6:00 AM | 2:30 PM |
| PERSON8 | Jazmyn Winters | Loader | 6:00 AM | 2:30 PM |
| PERSON9 | Larissa Barber | Loader | 6:00 AM | 2:30 PM |
| PERSON10 | Sabrina Jenkins | Loader | 6:00 AM | 2:30 PM |
| PERSON11 | Camille Weaver | Loader | 6:00 AM | 2:30 PM |
| PERSON12 | Billy Ellis | Loader | 5:00 AM | 1:30 PM |

=IF(OR(A5="Packer",A5="Loader"),"",VLOOKUP(A5,Users!$B$4:$E$31,3,FALSE))

| | C | D | E | F | G | H | I | J | K | L |
|---|---|---|---|---|---|---|---|---|---|---|
| | Total Cases | Time First Case | Time Last Case | Calc | Hour | Min | Sec | Worked Time | Work Time Calc 24 | Start Time |
| | 236 | | | | | | | | | |
| | 143 | 6:13:28 AM | 2:14:43 PM | 8:01:15 | 8 | 1 | 15 | 8.02 | 8.02 | 6:00:00 AM |

The only difference in the formula for end time is the return column is 4 instead of 3.

Start Time Formula

=IF(OR(A5="Packer",A5="Loader"),"",VLOOKUP(A5,Users!$B$4:$E$31,3,FALSE))

End Time Formula

=IF(OR(A5="Packer",A5="Loader"),"",VLOOKUP(A5,Users!$B$4:$E$31,4,FALSE))

To create the work schedule look up table a combination of techniques was utilized. The various work schedules are set up in a table called work schedules.

A Data Validation Drop Down was created to pull in the designated shift based on start time. A VLOOKUP was used to pull in the end time based on the start time selected and referencing the work schedule table.

| UserID | Name | Role | Start Time | End Time |
|--------|------|------|------------|----------|
| PERSON1 | Tristin Castillo | Loader | 4:00 AM | 12:30 PM |
| PERSON2 | Kamari Hayden | Loader | | 1:30 PM |
| PERSON3 | Maddox Terry | Loader | 4:00 AM | 2:30 PM |
| PERSON4 | Carmen Swanson | Loader | 5:00 AM | 2:30 PM |
| PERSON5 | Rhys Bates | Loader | 6:00 AM | 2:30 PM |
| PERSON6 | Miles Duncan | Loader | 7:00 AM | 2:30 PM |
| PERSON7 | Shawn Mcconnell | Loader | 8:00 AM | 2:30 PM |
| PERSON8 | Jazmyn Winters | Loader | 3:00 PM | 2:30 PM |
| PERSON9 | Larissa Barber | Loader | 4:00 PM | 2:30 PM |
| PERSON10 | Sabrina Jenkins | Loader | 5:00 PM | 2:30 PM |
| PERSON11 | Camille Weaver | Loader | 6:00 PM | 2:30 PM |
| PERSON12 | Billy Ellis | Loader | 5:00 AM | 1:30 PM |
| PERSON13 | Juliana Mason | Loader | 6:00 AM | 2:30 PM |

| Work Schedules | | |
|-------|-----|-------|
| Start | End | Hours |
| 4:00 AM | 12:30 PM | 8:30:00 |
| 5:00 AM | 1:30 PM | 8:30:00 |
| 6:00 AM | 2:30 PM | 8:30:00 |
| 7:00 AM | 3:30 PM | 8:30:00 |
| 8:00 AM | 4:30 PM | 8:30:00 |
| 3:00 PM | 11:30 PM | 8:30:00 |
| 4:00 PM | 12:30 AM | 8:30:00 |
| 5:00 PM | 1:30 AM | 8:30:00 |
| 6:00 PM | 2:30 AM | 8:30:00 |

The last elements of the daily summary table are calculation of the minutes from shift start to first transaction and then the last transaction to official end of shift or clock out time. This can help identify efficiency opportunities, A similar formula was utilized; the difference between the two times was calculated and then multiplied by 1440 to convert it to a decimal version of minutes.

The overtime indicator is an IF statement that compares the actual clock out or end time to the shift end time.

| Time to First Transaction | Last vs Clock Time | Overtime? |
|-----|-----|-----|
| 13.5 | -15 | |
| 11.3 | 103 | Yes |
| 56.4 | 137 | Yes |
| 59.4 | 143 | Yes |
| 11.8 | 82 | Yes |
| 11.7 | -13 | |
| 19.7 | -12 | |
| 19.4 | -11 | |

To allow for days with more people working, the formulas and formats were calculated down. It can be seen after conducting that step that when the name field is blank and there are no entries the formulas give errors or 0 values. The if statements looking for blanks or errors and then returning a blank will be added to the front of every formula. While this can be somewhat tedious it is a valuable step to clean up the daily summary table. Once the formula is created for one cell it can be copied and inserted directly to another formula. This can help save time finalizing the formulas.

| Date | 7/11/2023 | | | | | | | | | | | | | | |
|---|---|---|---|---|---|---|---|---|---|---|---|---|---|---|---|
| Row Labels | First | Total Cases | Time First Case | Time Last Case | Calc | Hour | Min | Sec | Worked Time | Work Time Calc 24 | Start Time | End Time | Time to First Transaction | Last vs Clock Time | Overtime? |
| Loader | 1 | 124 | | | | | | | | | | | | | |
| Billy Ellis | 1 | 124 | 6:12:41 AM | 2:18:49 PM | 8:06:08 | 8 | 6 | 8 | 8.10 | 8.10 | 5:00:00 AM | 1:30:00 PM | 72.7 | 49 | Yes |
| Camille Weaver | 1 | 50 | 6:37:58 AM | 2:17:53 PM | 7:39:55 | 7 | 39 | 55 | 7.67 | 7.67 | 6:00:00 AM | 2:30:00 PM | 38.0 | -12 | |
| Carmen Swanson | 1 | 92 | 6:49:03 AM | 2:03:24 PM | 7:14:21 | 7 | 14 | 21 | 7.24 | 7.24 | 6:00:00 AM | 2:30:00 PM | 49.1 | -27 | |
| Juliana Mccann | 1 | 88 | 6:58:30 AM | 2:17:49 PM | 7:19:19 | 7 | 19 | 19 | 7.32 | 7.32 | 6:00:00 AM | 2:30:00 PM | 58.5 | 12 | |
| Kamari Hayden | 1 | 51 | 6:26:08 AM | 2:15:47 PM | 7:49:39 | 7 | 49 | 39 | 7.83 | 7.83 | 5:00:00 AM | 1:30:00 PM | 86.1 | 46 | Yes |
| Maddox Terry | 1 | 85 | 6:42:27 AM | 2:07:18 PM | 7:24:51 | 7 | 24 | 51 | 7.41 | 7.41 | 6:00:00 AM | 2:30:00 PM | 42.5 | 23 | |
| Miles Duncan | 1 | 55 | 6:24:43 AM | 2:10:41 PM | 7:45:58 | 7 | 45 | 58 | 7.77 | 7.77 | 6:00:00 AM | 2:30:00 PM | 24.7 | -19 | |
| Rhys Bates | 1 | 14 | 7:01:08 AM | 1:56:36 PM | 6:55:28 | 6 | 55 | 28 | 6.92 | 6.92 | 6:00:00 AM | 2:30:00 PM | 61.1 | -33 | |
| Sabrina Jenkins | 1 | 39 | 6:14:22 AM | 1:53:22 PM | 7:39:00 | 7 | 39 | 0 | 7.65 | 7.65 | 6:00:00 AM | 2:30:00 PM | 14.4 | -37 | |
| Shawn Mcconnell | 1 | 67 | 6:29:50 AM | 1:56:01 PM | 7:26:11 | 7 | 26 | 11 | 7.44 | 7.44 | 6:00:00 AM | 2:30:00 PM | 29.8 | -34 | |
| Tristin Castillo | 1 | 51 | 7:46:40 AM | 2:15:58 PM | 6:29:18 | 6 | 29 | 18 | 6.49 | 6.49 | 4:00:00 AM | 12:30:00 PM | 226.7 | 106 | Yes |
| | | | 12:00:00 AM | 12:00:00 AM | 0:00:00 | 0 | 0 | 0 | 0.00 | 0.00 | #N/A | #N/A | #N/A | #N/A | #N/A |
| | | | 12:00:00 AM | 12:00:00 AM | 0:00:00 | 0 | 0 | 0 | 0.00 | 0.00 | #N/A | #N/A | #N/A | #N/A | #N/A |
| | | | 12:00:00 AM | 12:00:00 AM | 0:00:00 | 0 | 0 | 0 | 0.00 | 0.00 | #N/A | #N/A | #N/A | #N/A | #N/A |
| | | | 12:00:00 AM | 12:00:00 AM | 0:00:00 | 0 | 0 | 0 | 0.00 | 0.00 | #N/A | #N/A | #N/A | #N/A | #N/A |
| | | | 12:00:00 AM | 12:00:00 AM | 0:00:00 | 0 | 0 | 0 | 0.00 | 0.00 | #N/A | #N/A | #N/A | #N/A | #N/A |
| | | | 12:00:00 AM | 12:00:00 AM | 0:00:00 | 0 | 0 | 0 | 0.00 | 0.00 | #N/A | #N/A | #N/A | #N/A | #N/A |
| | | | 12:00:00 AM | 12:00:00 AM | 0:00:00 | 0 | 0 | 0 | 0.00 | 0.00 | #N/A | #N/A | #N/A | #N/A | #N/A |
| | | | 12:00:00 AM | 12:00:00 AM | 0:00:00 | 0 | 0 | 0 | 0.00 | 0.00 | #N/A | #N/A | #N/A | #N/A | #N/A |
| | | | 12:00:00 AM | 12:00:00 AM | 0:00:00 | 0 | 0 | 0 | 0.00 | 0.00 | #N/A | #N/A | #N/A | #N/A | #N/A |

=IF(A4="","",IF(OR(A4="Packer",A4="Loader"),"",SUMIFS(ReportPull[[#All],[Start Time]],ReportPull[[#All],[Sequence]],'Daily Summary'!B4,ReportPull[[#All],[Date]],'Daily Summary'!$B$1,ReportPull[[#All],[Name]],'Daily Summary'!A4)))

The addition to the formula can be seen above. The statement was added to the beginning and then one additional parenthesis was added. The formulas shown below has the IFERROR addition.

=IFERROR(IF(OR(A5="Packer",A5="Loader"),"",(D5-L5)*1440),"")

The last step for the formatting of the daily summary table, will be to hide unnecessary columns and add a slicer for the date.

Columns will be inserted to the left to allow room for the slicer.

| Date | 7/11/2023 | | | | | | | | | | | | | | |
|---|---|---|---|---|---|---|---|---|---|---|---|---|---|---|---|
| Row Labels | First | Total Cases | Time First Case | Time Last Case | Calc | Hour | Min | Sec | Worked Time | Work Time Calc 24 | Start Time | End Time | Time to First Transaction | Last vs Clock Time | Overtime? |
| ⊟ Loader | 1 | 124 | | | | | | | | | | | | | |
| Billy Ellis | 1 | 124 | 6:12:41 AM | 2:18:25 PM | 8:05:44 | 8 | 5 | 44 | 8.10 | 8.10 | 5:00:00 AM | 1:30:00 PM | 73 | 48 | Yes |
| Camille Weaver | 1 | 50 | 6:37:58 AM | 2:16:24 PM | 7:38:26 | 7 | 38 | 26 | 7.64 | 7.64 | 6:00:00 AM | 2:30:00 PM | 38 | -14 | |
| Carmen Swanson | 1 | 92 | 6:49:03 AM | 2:02:05 PM | 7:13:02 | 7 | 13 | 2 | 7.22 | 7.22 | 6:00:00 AM | 2:30:00 PM | 49 | -28 | |
| Juliana Mccann | 1 | 88 | 6:58:30 AM | 2:16:33 PM | 7:18:03 | 7 | 18 | 3 | 7.30 | 7.30 | 6:00:00 AM | 2:30:00 PM | 59 | -13 | |
| Kamari Hayden | 1 | 51 | 6:26:08 AM | 2:12:31 PM | 7:46:23 | 7 | 46 | 23 | 7.77 | 7.77 | 5:00:00 AM | 1:30:00 PM | 86 | 43 | Yes |
| Maddox Terry | 1 | 85 | 6:42:27 AM | 2:05:41 PM | 7:23:14 | 7 | 23 | 14 | 7.39 | 7.39 | 6:00:00 AM | 2:30:00 PM | 42 | -24 | |
| Miles Duncan | 1 | 55 | 6:24:43 AM | 2:09:43 PM | 7:45:00 | 7 | 45 | 0 | 7.75 | 7.75 | 6:00:00 AM | 2:30:00 PM | 25 | -20 | |
| Rhys Bates | 1 | 34 | 7:01:08 AM | 1:56:00 PM | 6:54:52 | 6 | 54 | 52 | 6.91 | 6.91 | 6:00:00 AM | 2:30:00 PM | 61 | -34 | |
| Sabrina Jenkins | 1 | 39 | 6:14:22 AM | 1:52:50 PM | 7:38:28 | 7 | 38 | 28 | 7.64 | 7.64 | 6:00:00 AM | 2:30:00 PM | 14 | -37 | |
| Shawn Mcconnell | 1 | 67 | 6:29:50 AM | 1:55:24 PM | 7:25:34 | 7 | 25 | 34 | 7.43 | 7.43 | 6:00:00 AM | 2:30:00 PM | 30 | -35 | |
| Tristin Castillo | 1 | 51 | 7:46:40 AM | 2:08:47 PM | 6:22:07 | 6 | 22 | 7 | 6.37 | 6.37 | 4:00:00 AM | 12:30:00 PM | 227 | 99 | Yes |

The resulting sheet can be seen below.

| Date | 7/10/2023 | | | | | | | | | |
|---|---|---|---|---|---|---|---|---|---|---|
| Row Labels | First | Total Cases | Time First Case | Time Last Case | Time Making Transactions | Start Time | End Time | Time to First Transaction | Last vs Clock Time | Overtime? |
| ⊟ Packer | 1 | 236 | | | | | | | | |
| Eden Meadows | 1 | 143 | 6:13:28 AM | 2:08:12 PM | 7.91 | 6:00:00 AM | 2:30:00 PM | 13 | -22 | |
| Ellis Caldwell | 1 | 147 | 5:11:16 AM | 3:12:09 PM | 10.01 | 5:00:00 AM | 1:30:00 PM | 11 | 102 | Yes |
| Kaylyn Leach | 1 | 145 | 4:56:25 AM | 2:45:51 PM | 9.82 | 4:00:00 AM | 12:30:00 PM | 56 | 136 | Yes |
| Laney Floyd | 1 | 236 | 4:59:24 AM | 2:52:51 PM | 9.89 | 4:00:00 AM | 12:30:00 PM | 59 | 143 | Yes |
| Maverick Dixon | 1 | 214 | 5:11:46 AM | 2:46:48 PM | 9.58 | 5:00:00 AM | 1:30:00 PM | 12 | 77 | Yes |
| Meadow Donovan | 1 | 137 | 5:11:42 AM | 1:07:53 PM | 7.94 | 5:00:00 AM | 1:30:00 PM | 12 | -22 | |
| Nigel Mayer | 1 | 83 | 6:19:42 AM | 2:13:10 PM | 7.89 | 6:00:00 AM | 2:30:00 PM | 20 | -17 | |
| Steve Anderson | 1 | 116 | 6:19:21 AM | 2:17:00 PM | 7.96 | 6:00:00 AM | 2:30:00 PM | 19 | -13 | |

Date slicer:
| Date |
|---|
| 7/10/2023 |
| 7/11/2023 |
| 7/12/2023 |
| 7/13/2023 |

The next step will be to add a VBA Macro to email the report.

The visual below shows the location that the VBA code should be copy and pasted into. It should be on the Worksheet section.

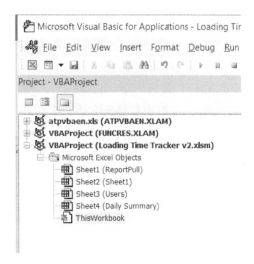

The VBA code for the Macro is shown on the next page with the main customized fields highlighted. If it is desired to not show the current date in the subject line, remove the code highlighted in pink.

CC and BCC can also be added, as well as, modifications to font type an size in the HTML portion of the code.

It is often a good idea to get the code running and then make modifications one at a time. This can help minimize troubleshooting time.

A button or object can then be added to the spreadsheet and assign the macro to it.

```vba
Sub send_email_with_table_as_pic()

Dim OutApp As Object
Dim OutMail As Object
Dim table As Range
Dim pic As Picture
Dim ws As Worksheet
Dim wordDoc
Dim dtToday As Date
dtToday = Date


Set OutApp = CreateObject("Outlook.Application")
Set OutMail = OutApp.CreateItem(0)

'grab table, convert to image, and cut
Set ws = ThisWorkbook.Sheets("Daily Summary")
Set table = ws.Range("C1:R30")
ws.Activate
table.Copy
Set pic = ws.Pictures.Paste
pic.Cut

'create email message
On Error Resume Next
  With OutMail
    .to = "enteremail@email.com"
    .CC = ""
    .BCC = ""
    .Subject = "Daily Summary Report " & dtToday
    .Display

    Set wordDoc = OutMail.GetInspector.WordEditor
      With wordDoc.Range
        .PasteandFormat wdChartPicture
        .insertParagraphAfter
        .insertParagraphAfter
        .InsertAfter "Thank you,"
        .insertParagraphAfter
        .InsertAfter "Department Supervisor"
      End With

    .HTMLBody = "<BODY style = font-size:11pt; font-family:Calibri>" & _
      "Hi Team, <p> Please see table below: <p>" & .HTMLBody
  End With
  On Error GoTo 0

Set OutApp = Nothing
Set OutMail = Nothing

End Sub
```

Module 15

The completed spreadsheet summary page and resulting email is shown below:

| Send Email | Date | | |
|---|---|---|---|
| | 7/10/2023 | | |
| | 7/11/2023 | | |
| | 7/12/2023 | | |
| | 7/13/2023 | | |

Send

| To | enteremail@email.com |
|---|---|
| Cc | |

Subject | Daily Summary Report 11/13/2023

Hi Team,

Please see table below:

| Date | 7/10/2023 | | | | | | | | | |
|---|---|---|---|---|---|---|---|---|---|---|
| Row Labels | First | Total Cases | Time First Case | Time Last Case | Time Making Transactions | Start Time | End Time | Time to First Transaction | Last vs Clock Time | Overtime? |
| Packer | 1 | 236 | | | | | | | | |
| Eden Meadows | 1 | 143 | 6:13:28 AM | 2:08:12 PM | 7.91 | 6:00:00 AM | 2:30:00 PM | 13 | -22 | |
| Ellis Caldwell | 1 | 147 | 5:11:16 AM | 3:12:09 PM | 10.01 | 5:00:00 AM | 1:30:00 PM | 11 | 102 | Yes |
| Kaylyn Leach | 1 | 145 | 4:56:25 AM | 2:45:51 PM | 9.82 | 4:00:00 AM | 12:30:00 PM | 56 | 136 | Yes |
| Laney Floyd | 1 | 236 | 4:59:24 AM | 2:52:51 PM | 9.89 | 4:00:00 AM | 12:30:00 PM | 59 | 143 | Yes |
| Maverick Dixon | 1 | 214 | 5:11:46 AM | 2:46:48 PM | 9.58 | 5:00:00 AM | 1:30:00 PM | 12 | 77 | Yes |
| Meadow Donovan | 1 | 137 | 5:11:42 AM | 1:07:53 PM | 7.94 | 5:00:00 AM | 1:30:00 PM | 12 | -22 | |
| Nigel Mayer | 1 | 83 | 6:19:42 AM | 2:13:10 PM | 7.89 | 6:00:00 AM | 2:30:00 PM | 20 | -17 | |
| Steve Anderson | 1 | 116 | 6:19:21 AM | 2:17:00 PM | 7.96 | 6:00:00 AM | 2:30:00 PM | 19 | -13 | |

Thank you,
Department Supervisor

In order to trend the data over time, the daily data is copy and pasted to a separate sheet named "Copy Paste" using a Macro. The only addition that is needed to the sheet is the date of that report. Column S was used to pull the date from the pivot table filter using the $ to freeze the cell to always be D1. This is a good example of absolute reference usage. The column was then hidden from the daily summary view but is included in the range that the macro copies.

The macro is relatively straight forward and could almost be made from recording the steps to copy paste to a new sheet except for the VBA code that takes the data and puts after the last row which is designate below for future reference.

```
Range("A4").Select
  MaxRows = Cells(Rows.Count, "A").End(xlUp).Row

   Range("A" & MaxRows + 1).Select

  Selection.PasteSpecial Paste:=xlPasteValues, Operation:=xlNone, SkipBlanks _
    :=False, Transpose:=False
```

The date formula carried to all cells is shown below.

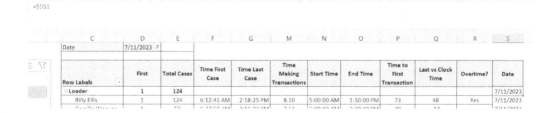

The Copy Paste to new sheet VBA code is shown below with the customized parts highlighted in yellow.

```
Sub SaveCopyPaste()
'
' SaveCopyPaste Macro
'

'

    Range("c4:s30").Select
    Selection.Copy
    Sheets("Copy Paste").Select
    Range("A4").Select
    MaxRows = Cells(Rows.Count, "A").End(xlUp).Row

      Range("A" & MaxRows + 1).Select


    Selection.PasteSpecial Paste:=xlPasteValues, Operation:=xlNone, SkipBlanks _
        :=False, Transpose:=False
    Sheets("Daily Summary").Select
    ActiveWindow.SmallScroll Down:=-8
    Range("L1").Select
    Application.CutCopyMode = False


End Sub
```

The Copy Paste sheet will be used to create trend for the various loader efficiency metrics. In review of the copy paste data, it was realized that it would be possible to generate duplicates so a series of functions were put together to remove duplicates after each copy paste.

To facilitate the auto filling of formulas the Copy Paste sheet was converted to a table using the "Format as Table" Icon.

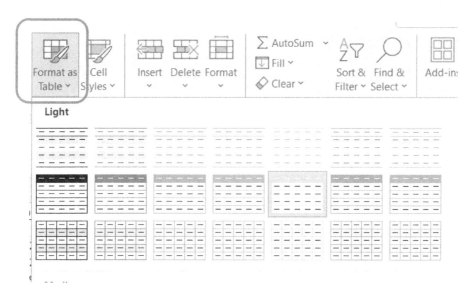

A concatenate or join field was added to create a filed that combines the Name, First Transaction time and Date with the reality that there should not be duplicates of that combination of fields. That was performed with the & symbol.

=[@[Row Labels]]&[@[Time First Case]]&[@Date]

Then Removing duplicates was recorded using Macro Record and the resulting VBA code was copy and pasted on to the copy paste macro. Only some sheet and cell designations were added manually.

The additional code is shown below.

```
Sheets("Copy Paste").Select
    Range("R2").Select

    Range("A2").Select
    ActiveSheet.Range("Table2[#All]").RemoveDuplicates Columns:=18,
Header:= _
        xlYes

    Sheets("Daily Summary").Select
```

The following graphs were set up using the copy paste data set.  It can be seen that the trends include slicers for individual people and a timeline for the average cases per hour.  There is a summary table showing average time between last transaction and shift end time.

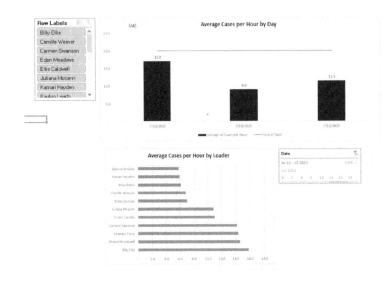

A refresh macro was created by recording the steps to refresh the pivot tables. This includes refreshing the daily summary tables. The filters were removed, put on and removed to ensure that all were removed. Then each pivot table was selected, and the Refresh option was chosen in Data > Refresh.

There were also some formatting set and the macro can be reviewed to see the how the code looks for formatting column widths.

It is also possible to standardize options by Right Clicking and going into Pivot Table Options. To ensure that any error values show up as blank check that checkbox and uncheck Autofit column widths after update to keep the cell width formatting.

A single refresh vs refresh all is used so that it only refreshes the selected tables vs all updatable contents which would include tables that have connections and all pivot tables.

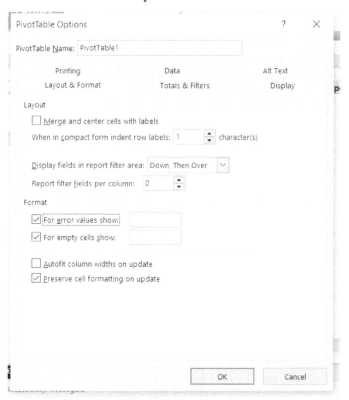

The next steps will be showing how to link the Microsoft Excel content to Microsoft PowerPoint and have them update when new data is available.

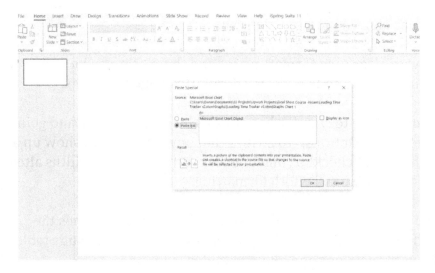

A new day of data will be added to the folder, and a Daily Summary Refresh macro was created recording steps to refresh the data pull and refresh the pivot tables. All filters are removed as part of the refresh so that the refresh can fully execute.

The new data will be added and daily report can be run and emailed for that day. The pivot tables and graphs can be updated on the graph tab and then when opening the power point with links, click the button update links to refresh with new data. If just opening to look at the file, click cancel and it will open.

The PowerPoint can be saved with a different name and the links can be broken or it can be saved as a PDF.

The PowerPoint dialogue box is shown. Cancel to open without refreshing, Update Links to refresh with new data.

The file with links can be saved as a master file and each time it is updated it can be saved with a different name and the links can be broken in the menu below or the file can be saved as a PDF. This saves an issues with sharing the file and the file looking for linked data.

Select Break Links to remove the links from the PowerPoint in the copy.

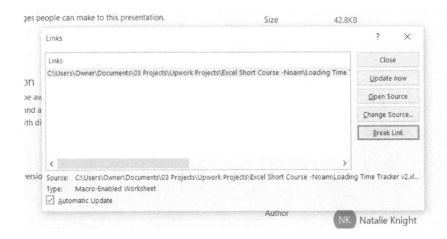

The resulting slide is shown below.

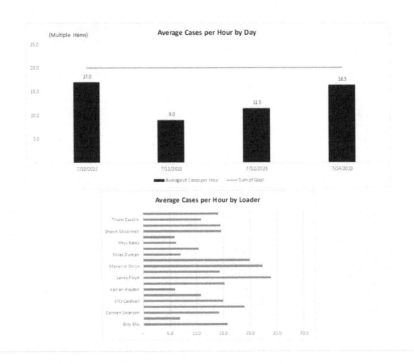

Another feature that was added to this use case to help the user was formatting of the USERIDs for easy copy paste into the system where the data was being downloaded each day. The system required that the data be delimited horizontally with a semicolon in between. The TEXTJOIN formula along with a simple copy macro was used to accomplish this.

On the Users sheet the TextJoin formula was added to join with a semicolon the values in cells A5 to A31. To test the copy within a spreadsheet, paste as values.

$$=TEXTJOIN("; ",TRUE,A5:A31)$$

PERSON1; PERSON2; PERSON3; PERSON4; PERSON5; PERSON6; PERSON7;

**Copy Users**

# Summary: Module 15

This module contains a use case that combines many of the aspects learned in order to create a spreadsheet that can produce a daily summary report in a timely manner.

Microsoft Query was used to pull in the data that resides in separate excel files by date. As new dates are added to the folder the data table that contains the raw data can be updated. The update is processed through a Data > Refresh step which is the same steps for updating pivot tables.

The data comes downloaded from a system and some formatting formulas needed to be utilize. There were several examples of performing calculations with date / time style data and summary tables and charts were created.

A macro was used to refresh the data and save each date to a copy paste sheet. This copy paste sheet has historical data and can be used to trend the process output over time. The macro also contains some lines of code that removed duplicates. This section of code was added by recording the removal of duplicates and pasting the resulting code along with the other macros.

# Module 16

- Dashboards
- Hyperlinks

Dashboards are a popular method of summarizing related data in an efficient and visual appealing manner. There are various formats of dashboards that can be created in Microsoft Excel. This section will highlight a few different concepts.

The concepts related Tables, Formulas, Graphs, Macros, Pivot Tables, Formatting and Hyperlinks all come together with Dashboarding. Company Logos and customized colors are usually added to enhance visual appeal.

The first example use case is a Human Resource Staffing and Recruiting Dashboard. Each element will be explained.

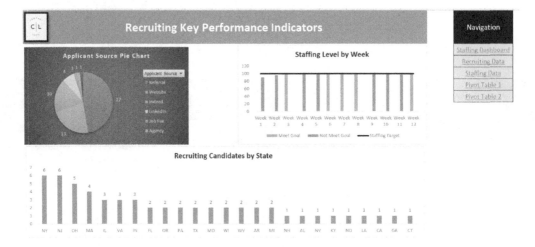

The custom colors can be set by selecting the desired cell or cells and navigating to format. When choosing the color go to custom and enter either the Hex code or RGB numbers. This method can also be used to determine what color a currently format cell has in order to use later.

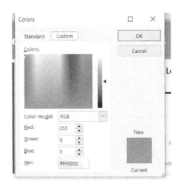

Navigation

Staffing Dashboard
Recruiting Data
Staffing Data
Pivot Table 1
Pivot Table 2

Once the color scheme is selected which in this case was red and black primarily. The Company Logo placeholder was added, and the first row was sized to create a header. Columns in row one were merged and centered to create a header that fits on the computer screen at 100% setting. The pie chart was created with a pivot table using applicant sources and a count column. A preselect color scheme was selected to give it the darker background. Field buttons were right clicked and hidden.

The Recruiting Candidates by State bar graph was made by creating a pivot table with State in the rows and sum of a count field to total number by state. The pivot table was sorted high to low using the sort Z to A option and the data labels were added to the outside end.

The red and green bar chart for staffing level was created using and if statement and creating two different series. One series populates if the value meets the goal, if not a blank, and the other series populates if the value does not meet goal. The two series are plotted together, and the color format is changed. The series that does not meet goal is colored red and the series that is set to populate if goal is met, is colored with a green format.

The Navigation pane is set up with text and hyperlinks in each cell to the corresponding page. Since the Recruiting sheet contains the main navigation page, there is no navigation link listed to in the list. However, each sheet has a return button that returns back to this dashboard main page.

Module 16

The set up for this style graph with two series and IF statements are shown below.

| Week | Staffing Target | Staffing Level | Meet Goal | Not Meet Goal |
|---|---|---|---|---|
| Week 1 | 100 | 90 | =IF(C2>=B2,C2,"") | =IF(C2<B2,C2,"") |
| Week 2 | 100 | 95 | | 95 |
| Week 3 | 100 | 100 | 100 | |
| Week 4 | 100 | 99 | | 99 |
| Week 5 | 100 | 98 | | 98 |
| Week 6 | 100 | 101 | 101 | |
| Week 7 | 100 | 100 | 100 | |
| Week 8 | 100 | 100 | 100 | |
| Week 9 | 100 | 99 | | 99 |
| Week 10 | 100 | 98 | | 98 |
| Week 11 | 100 | 97 | | 97 |
| Week 12 | 100 | 100 | 100 | |

| Week | Staffing Target | Staffing Level | Meet Goal | Not Meet Goal |
|------|-----------------|----------------|-----------|---------------|
| Week 1 | 100 | 90 | | 90 |
| Week 2 | 100 | 95 | | 95 |
| Week 3 | 100 | 100 | 100 | |
| Week 4 | 100 | 99 | | 99 |
| Week 5 | 100 | 98 | | 98 |
| Week 6 | 100 | 101 | 101 | |
| Week 7 | 100 | 100 | 100 | |
| Week 8 | 100 | 100 | 100 | |
| Week 9 | 100 | 99 | | 99 |
| Week 10 | 100 | 98 | | 98 |
| Week 11 | 100 | 97 | | 97 |
| Week 12 | 100 | 100 | 100 | |

This sheet that contains the formulas and formatting for the conditional series bar chart is not part of the main navigation menu but does have the return hyperlink added to the arrow image.

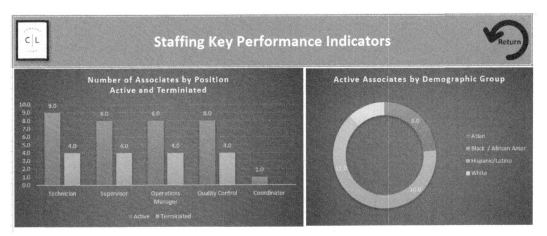

The staffing dashboard page follows the same color scheme and logo design as the main page. It was created by right click on the recruiting dashboard sheet and creating a copy within the same workbook. The sheet tab was renamed and colored. The title name was changed and the return arrow image with hyperlink to main dashboard page was added to header. The bar chart is a count of Active and Terminated associates. The pivot table used to create this chart has the position listed in the rows and the status of active or terminated in the columns. A text field was selected to count in the values. When choosing a column for counting, you must ensure that it has values in ever cell where appropriate. The formatting of the bar chart was created using a pre-set format theme.

The chart on the right is a doughnut chart and is part of the pie chart menu. It is showing the category of demographic group by active associates and was set up and filtered in a pivot table. Formatting was also a pre-set format and was selected to match the bar chart.

The two data sheets are on separate tabs and house the raw data. They both have a navigation to the main dashboard page and are the source data for the pivot tables.

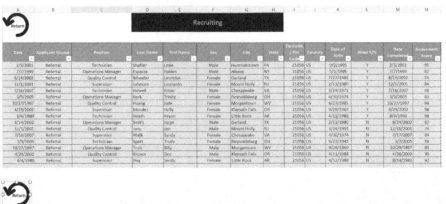

The Pivot Table pages are used as workspaces to generate the charts and visuals. As new data becomes available on the data sheets, the pivot tables are refreshed, and the corresponding graphs will update as well.  They are connected to the main page dashboard and will update, as well. Both Pivot table pages have navigation back to the main page.

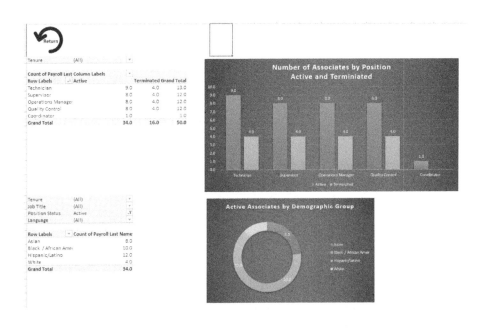

This first dashboard example demonstrates that by combining some basic concepts, a dashboard can be created in a straightforward manner. As the data is updated the pivot tables and charts are also updated. This primarily used pivot tables, charts, formatting and hyperlinks to create the dashboard.

The next example that will be reviewed is the shell of a dashboard template that houses increased amount of navigation and data. This file can be used as a simple template.

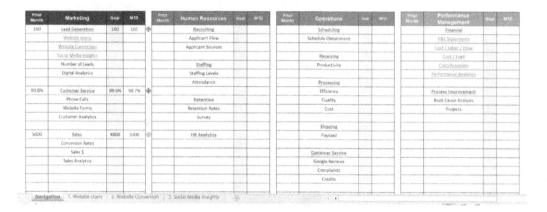

The structure of this dashboard template allows for a large volume of data organized on one main navigation page. They are grouped into four process categories. There is a header for a group of metrics and then each metric has a specific page. Number of the sheets with the title helps with organization.

There is a hyperlink created from the words to the number sheet. That sheet can contain data and graphs for that metric. Each metric sheet would have a navigation back to the main page.

There are also some summary numbers with icon set example being used to compare month to month. The numbers can be pulled into a table of this nature using SUMIFS, AVERAGEIFS, and COUNTIFS from the data sheets. Many of those formulas will be similar and they will just reference different columns and cells.

The third dashboard example has a Key Performance Indicator (KPI) page for a process that has multiple locations and a large process with many steps. This KPI tile page that has both dynamic and interactive features.

Starting with the top left corner, a drop down exists in order to filter the data in the KPI tiles by location. This drop down was created using data validation with the source data in column Y of the same sheet. Directly under the location selector drop down is a place where the date range can be entered. This also allows for viewing the KPI data summary over different time periods.

The KPI tiles were created by sizing rows and columns to be able to create the three parts of the tile. One part is pulling a summary of that process metric, the other is a label indicating what metric is included in the tile. The third component is a navigation link to a page containing details and trends about that metric.

The data is pulled into the tile by using SUMIFS, COUNTIFS, and AVERAGIFS depending on the metric. Conditional formatting is used to color it red or green depending on if it is meeting a goal or target.

The goal values for the conditional formatting was entered directly into the formula section vs referencing another cell. The conditional formats have three rules and the and the stop if true checkbox was used for the cases where there is no data.

When there is no data, an error would return in the calculation and instead of returning a blank with the iferror statement the word "none" was used. As it is a text value, it also needs to be within double quotes. All KPI metrics have the IFERROR formula returning "none".

Below shows and example of the none return.

Each process step and corresponding KPI metric has two sheets, one for the data and one for a dashboard for that metric. The data was created with data pulls using Power Query coming from a database.

The main page is shown below is not utilized for visualization but more for organization and data management. The hyperlinks go to each of the different sheets.

The buttons are refresh macros that perform a refresh of the data pulls as well as the pivot tables. At the end of the refresh macro there is VBA code to enter the date and time that the code was executed. The code for the date / time stamp is shown below. In this case, instead of referring to the cell as a letter and number, it is the position with Cell(R, C).

```
Sheets("Main").Select
Range("F8").Select


Cells(3, 6).Value = Now
```

The data and dashboard structure and contents are demonstrated using Step 10 of the process.

The data sheet is set up as a Power Query data pull from a database. It can be refreshed using Data Refresh. The dynamic table design is used, and additional columns were added to include formulas such as extracting the year, month and week of the data point.

Extra rows were inserted at the top to allow for navigation hyperlinks and date, location information. It pulls the data in from the main page, and they are showing for reference and consistency.

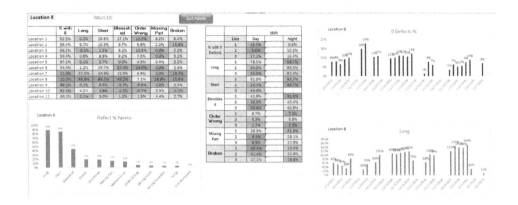

The dashboard has several familiar elements utilized together. The table in the upper left-hand corner shows each location for that particular metric. There are different measures calculated for each location which are the columns of the table. SUMFIS, AVERAGEIFS, and COUTNIFS was used to pull in the summary number. The Microsoft Excel conditional formatting color scales were used to create the relative colors. Different ones were used depending on if red was good or red was bad.

The charts are created from static tables not pivot tables in this case. The date range is included based on a flag formula that puts a one (1) if the date value is in between the selected range on the main dashboard. When the main dashboard is updated, the date range updates and SUMIFS, AVERAGEIFS, and COUNTIFS formulas are used to pull in the values for the different dates. This will then update the corresponding charts.

While this type of dashboard with large process contains a lot of formulas and details, many of them are similar and when building it and setting things up, copying and modifying techniques can be utilized.

The sort macro can be seen below. This macro was created by recording the steps and then assigning it to a sort labeled button.

```
Sub sortpareto()
'
' sortpareto Macro
'

'

  Sheets("Step 10 Pareto").Select
  Range("Q4:R32").Select
  ActiveWorkbook.Worksheets("Step 10 Pareto").Sort.SortFields.Clear
  ActiveWorkbook.Worksheets("Step 10 Pareto").Sort.SortFields.Add Key:=Range( _
    "R5:R16"), SortOn:=xlSortOnValues, Order:=xlDescending, DataOption:= _
    xlSortNormal
  With ActiveWorkbook.Worksheets("Step 10 Pareto").Sort
    .SetRange Range("Q4:R32")
    .Header = xlYes
    .MatchCase = False
    .Orientation = xlTopToBottom
    .SortMethod = xlPinYin
    .Apply
  End With
  Range("Q2").Select
  Sheets("Step 10 Dashboard").Select
End Sub
```

# Summary: Module 16

Module 16, Dashboarding, demonstrated with three examples how to make different styles of dashboards using a combination of principles and techniques. There is a high degree of customization options and navigate pages with hyperlinks facilitate the organization and makes moving around the sheets efficient.

The visualizations are combined to create informative summaries that can be dynamic or static in nature. In some cases, macros will be utilized to refresh and organize, while in other cases, more simplified formulas are used.

# Module 17

- Microsoft Excel Templates

Microsoft Excel has several premade templates that are available upon searching on the File > New menu and typing in the search box.

After gaining some familiarity and experience with Microsoft Excel, these templates can be very helpful as they can be used directly as they are or perhaps, they inspire a concept that you can build upon.

Another reality as you progress through the Excel journey is that often times it is not necessary to fully understand how or why something works, particularly with macros or complicated formulas. Just know that they are available and learning how to apply them within your application really helps the progression of your respective skill set. The same goes for templates. Take the concepts or the parts of the concepts and combine them with your own vision and abilities to create a solution.

As you continue to work with Microsoft Excel there will become an increasingly larger set of things that are understood and can be applied together in various combinations.

This section is highlighting some of the templates available that may be useful in your Microsoft Excel Journey.

Module 17

## Calendar

This calendar template is great as the user can enter the year and desired starting day of the week and the calendar is generated with each month on a separate sheet.

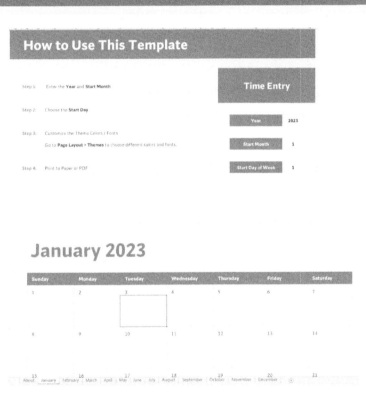

There is also the ability to type within a certain day to by adding text to that cell.

## Timesheet

The timesheet template is designed for a single person's time entry. It is pretty straightforward and upon entering the start and stop times will calculate the hours.

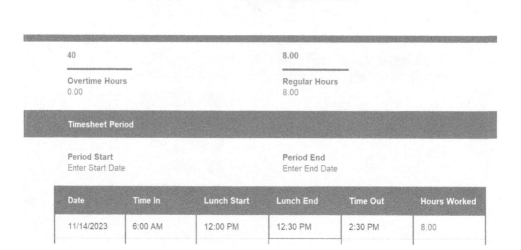

It allows for removing a lunch break, as well.

## Event Planner

The Event Planner Template includes some unique formatting options and includes both a checklist and expense planner.

There are four tabs included and customization would be relatively simple.

## Gantt Chart

Gantt charts are a great project management tool as it integrates milestones with timelines. This pre-made Microsoft Excel template allows for straightforward plugging in of customizable data.

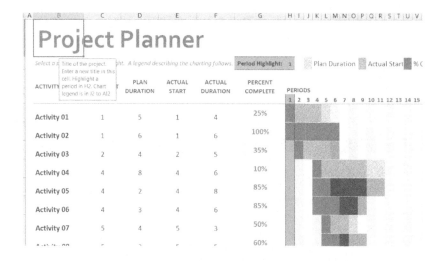

## Holiday Budget Planner

The Holiday Budget Planner allows for four different categories of expenses and creation of a budget for each item within that category. It utilizes color and visual shapes.

## To Do List

This creative To-Do list allows for task assignment to customized names and crosses off the task when it is marked complete.

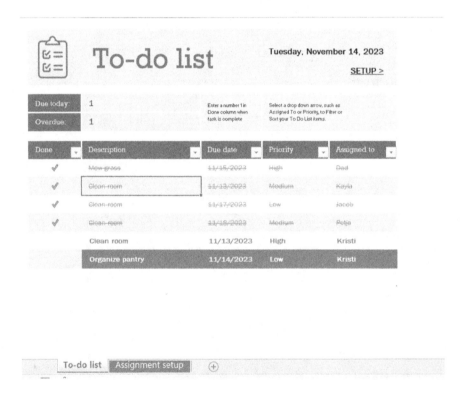

# Income Statement

This one-page income statement template is easy and straightforward to customize. It is sized for easy printing and calculations are part of the template.

Income statement 1 year1

## Income Statement

| | |
|---|---|
| Quinn Campbell | FYXX Q2 |
| Financial statements in U.S. dollars | |

### REVENUE

| | | |
|---|---|---|
| Gross sales | 500,654 | |
| Less: sales returns and allowances | | |
| Net sales | | $500,654 |

### COST OF GOODS SOLD

| | | |
|---|---|---|
| Beginning inventory | 123 | |
| Add: Purchases | 65 | |
| Freight-in | 2 | |
| Direct labor | 12 | |
| Indirect expenses | 5 | |
| Inventory available | 207 | |
| Less: ending inventory | 132 | |
| Cost of goods sold | | $75 |
| | | |
| Gross profit (loss) | | $500,579 |

### EXPENSES

## Job Candidate Tracker

This tracker is great for organizing recruiting efforts. It has contact information cells as well as clearly highlighted status.

While this template is specific to the recruiting process, the concept can be applied to many different process as a contact and status tracker.

Job candidates tracker1

## Mileage Log

The mileage log tracker has a very straightforward layout and the design is customized for a roadway theme.

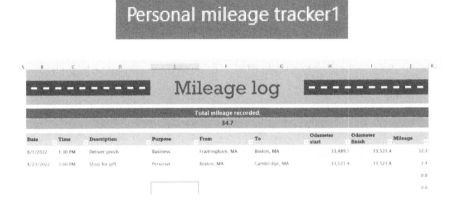

## Personal Budget Tracker

This is a great user friendly, customizable layout. It contains an information sheet with instructions on how to use the template.

# Profit and Loss Statement

The template is customizable including a place for a logo. The main categories are on separate sheets and are integrated into a summary dashboard page, shown below.

## Profit and Loss Statement with Sparkline

This is a great template for showing monthly trends combined in a table and then with an efficiently place sparkline for a quick visual indicator of the trend direction.

## Invoice Statement

Simple, straightforward template design for an invoice. Allows for customization of company information including logo.

Simple invoice1

# Company Logo

# INVOICE

| | |
|---|---|
| Invoice #: | 10654 |
| Invoice | 11/14/2023 |
| Job: | Wedding |

345 W Main
Los Angeles, CA 14151
P: 315-555-0195
F: 315-555-0105
elegantembrace@example.com

| | |
|---|---|
| Bill to: | Hailey Clark |
| Address: | 123 Avenue A, Burbank, CA 56789 |
| Phone: | 805-555-0185 |
| Fax: | NA |

| Item # | Description | Qty | Unit price | Discount | Price |
|---|---|---|---|---|---|
| A875 | Peonies | 35 | $1.05 | | $36.75 |
| K245 | Tulips | 25 | $2.00 | | $50.00 |
| U123 | Buttercup | 30 | $1.35 | | $40.50 |
| | | | | | |
| | | | | | |
| | | | | | |
| | | | | | |
| | | | | | |

| | |
|---|---|
| Invoice Subtotal | $127.25 |
| Tax Rate | 6.00% |
| Sales Tax | $7.64 |
| Deposit Received | $50.00 |
| **TOTAL** | $77.25 |

Please make all checks payable to Company Logo.
Total due in 30 days. Overdue accounts subject to a service charge of 1.5% per month.
elegantembrace@example.com | www.interestingsite.com

## Profit and Loss Statement

This template has the P&L Statement on one sheet for easy entry and fills in with formulas.

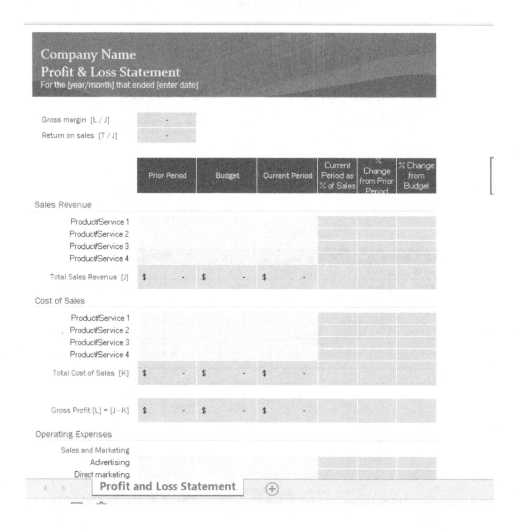

## Weekly Schedule Planner

Nice formatted, easy to use Microsoft Excel schedule planner. Great for customization, editing and keeping track of schedule electronically or in printed form.

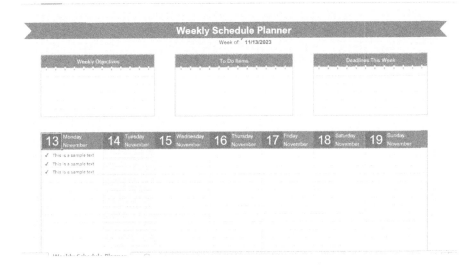

# Microsoft Excel Course: Conclusion

Congratulations! You have successfully completed the Microsoft Excel course designed at taking beginners through the fundamentals and with application to examples and case studies are able to perform advanced operations.

As you continue to work with Microsoft Excel you will continue to build on the skills obtained in the course. As you gain experience with different types of spreadsheets and interact with other individuals you will continue to pick up tricks and techniques.

Functionality continues to improve and as you continue this journey, you will too.

Enjoy yourself as you create and utilize the powerful and widely used application of Microsoft Excel!

Made in the USA
Las Vegas, NV
22 April 2024

88991746R00157